W9-CMN-226

AMERICAN
TALK

Where
Our Words
Came From

Random House New York

AMERICAN TALK

J. L. Dillard

Library of Congress Cataloging in Publication Data

Dillard, Joey Lee, 1924–
  American talk: where our words came from.

Bibliography: p.
Includes index.
1. English language in the United States.
2. English language—Slang.   3. Americanisms.
I. Title.
PE2846.D5   427'.9'73   76–10645
ISBN 0–394–40012–7

Manufactured in the United States of America

9 8 7 6 5 4 3 2

Contents

Acknowledgments

Students and colleagues at several universities have provided material for this book. Dr. Ian F. Hancock of the University of Texas, Austin, has been especially helpful with detailed information on little-known language varieties. Margie I. Dillard assisted in all stages of preparation of the manuscript.

The most important influences, however, have been the writings of scholars concerned with aspects of American English who work outside the linguistic mainstream. Among these, perhaps the most important is Ramon Adams, whose *Western Words* is the most useful guide one can find to the language of the cowboy and certain other frontier groups, and whose *The Rampaging Herd* is the best bibliography on the subject. Other material on the language of the pioneer is contained in the works of historians like Philip Ashton Rollins, Everett N. Dick, and Josiah Gregg. Walter McCulloch's *Woods Words* contains important information on the speech patterns of the Northwest.

Among books more explicitly concerned with linguistic matters, a few, generally overlooked by researchers, have proved to be invaluable. Brian Foster's *The Changing English Language* has material on the German influence on American English that made it unnecessary for me to deal with that topic and encouraged me to look rather to Dutch. Lilian Feinsilver's *The Taste of Yiddish* makes any further attempt to cope with the influence of Yiddish superfluous. Joanna Carver Colcord's *Sea Language Comes Ashore* treats nautical influences more thoroughly than any other work has done.

The Dictionary of Americanisms and the older *Dictionary of American English* (often strikingly similar in content) are, if not absolutely complete, near enough to discourage competition. Together with *The Oxford English Dictionary,* they are essential tools for anyone working in this field. In fact, unless a bibliographic attribution of another nature is made in the text, it should be assumed that any citation in this book comes from one of these sources. However, unless otherwise stated, all interpretations are my own, and divergences from long-accepted opinion are intentional.

Introduction

This book is part of a continuing effort to determine the origins of and influences on the language spoken in the United States of America. As such, it has a direct relationship to my two earlier books, *Black English* and *All-American English*. In those books I attempted to show how Pidgin English and the Creole that results when a pidgin becomes the native language of a group were of basic importance in separating American English from British. In this book, I carry that investigation farther by considering the detailed workings of language-contact influences on the vocabulary and phraseology of American English.

Methodologically, the book follows the premise that an earlier period can be best understood by examining the records of intelligent observers who were there. It does not assume that such observers were perfect, or that their descriptions were always comparable to those of modern social scientists. It does, however, insist that their observations be taken into account in any general picture. If a great number of eighteenth- and nineteenth-century observers recorded the speaking of Pidgin English by American Indians, it does not matter if some twentieth-century armchair theorist decides that a pidgin was never spoken in the continental United States. The evidence is there.

It is generally accepted that in the Americas some words were added to the English language, some were changed in meaning, and others retained archaic meanings that they lost in British English. But according to the conventional position, the "basic" grammatical structure of the English language was unaffected. Recently, however, the emphasis in linguistics has shifted to semantics, or the study of meaning, as the most important level of language. And the semantic change in American English, including as it does influences from many other languages, is marked. If semantic structure is more basic to language than inflectional endings, then American English has changed more, not less, than it would have if a few new inflectional endings (something like *we arop, you arel,* to accompany *I am, he is,* etc.) had been picked up.

Some of the familiar examples of semantic change are worth examining. It is well known, for example, that *corn* was a general term for grain in England, but in America it came to be applied, first in the phrase *Indian corn,* to what might otherwise have become *maize* in the colonies. In 1838, Harriet Martineau wrote:

> It occurred to me that some of our commonest English writing must bear a different meaning to Americans, and to us. All that is written about cornfields, for instance, must call up pictures in their minds quite unlike any that the poets intended to create. "Waving corn" is not the true description to them; and one can scarcely bring one's tongue to explain that it means "small grain." Their poetical attachments are naturally and reasonably to their Indian corn, a beautiful plant, worthy of all love and celebration. But the consequence is that we have not their sympathy about our sheaves, our harvest wain, our gleaners; for though they have that, their harvest *par excellence* is of corn-cobs, and their "small grain" bears about the same relation to poetry with them as turnips.

Anyone who has ever heard a class in sophomore literature snickering over Keats's line "She stood in tears amid the alien corn" knows that Martineau was not exaggerating.

Martineau's linguistic sensitivity allowed her to perceive that American English had been *differentiated* rather than corrupted. This is preferable, from a linguistic point of view, to making value judgments about "good" and "bad" language. Martineau is linguistically superior to Charles Dickens, who wrote in *American Notes* (1842) : "I need not tell you that the prevailing grammar [in America] is more than doubtful, and that the oddest vulgarisms are received idioms."

Dickens even went so far as to assert that American language forms were not intelligible to British visitors. In Chapter II of *American Notes* he reports that he did not understand what was meant when a waiter asked him if he wanted his dinner *right away.* He or any other Englishman would have understood the word *right* and the word *away.* What was wrong was the combination of the two. In the same author's *Martin Chuzzlewit* (Chapter XXVII), Martin does not understand the American Mrs. Hominy when she asks, "Where do you hail from?" There are other reports of the difficulty Englishmen of the period had with American expressions.

Today, when a more-or-less popular interpreter of culture tries to differentiate between American and British English (as most of them do at one time or another), he usually leans heavily on terms like *jargon* for American usage. Richard Freeman, reviewing *All-American English* in the New York *Post* for May 27, 1975, represented the tradition almost perfectly by asserting that we are not as coherent or as jargon-free as the "average literate Englishman," but that we manage to achieve a certain "dash and color" which can be compared to "Renaissance English" or "the language of Elizabeth [I]."

When a professional dialectologist goes about describing the differences between American and British English, he eschews terms like *jargon.* He stresses a few vocabulary items and ways of pronunciation as the major differences— a car's *bonnet* instead of *hood, chemist's* for *drugstore,* etc., and "ah" rather than "a" in *path, bath, dance, fancy.*

Most of us are not really convinced by the professional dialectologist—the difference just has to be greater than that. So unless we have to take a test on Dialectology 101 or a Ph.D. oral this semester, we go back to the impressions of the popular observer, which appeal to us without our being able to say exactly why. We *know* that the reviews in the (London) *Times Literary Supplement* have something that the reviews in the (New York) *Times Book Review* don't. But we don't always try to explain the difference.

Freeman's reference to Elizabethan English may be instructive, although not necessarily in the way one might expect. Anyone who has studied either Renaissance literature or the history of early modern English must be aware that Englishmen in the "great age" of English literature were not so confident of their own superiority. They were still somewhat servile toward foreign models—especially toward writers who had achieved the great feat of living a few centuries earlier. Renaissance Englishmen said things about the "rudeness" and "barbarousness" of English, and they worried about how to make it the equal of contemporary Romance languages. (There were even a few ambitious souls who dared to think of making it equal to Latin or Greek!) For the majority of sixteenth- and seventeenth-century Englishmen, the language of Shakespeare was no vehicle for great, permanent literature, but rather an inferior tool fit only for transient expression. From William Caxton, the fifteenth-century printer and translator, to Francis Bacon two hundred years later, important writers expressed reluctance to write in their native tongue and made elaborate excuses for using "this rude and comyn Englyssh." Many, like Roger Ascham in *Toxophilus* (1545), asserted that they stooped to English only because they wished to appeal to readers who would not be able to understand Latin.

Wholesale borrowings from other languages, most especially from French after the Norman Conquest, left English with a supply of terms like *timorosity, odible, jurate,* and *adminiculation.* These words were especially abundant in works of the Euphuistic style, which Shakespeare parodied beautifully in the speech of the pedant Holofernes in *Love's Labour's Lost:*

> I abhor such fanastical phanasimes, such insociable and point-devise companions, such rackers of orthographie . . .

When it comes to clichés and stale comparisons, nothing can approach the Elizabethan sonnet sequence, which features skin white as snow, eyes like stars, and teeth like pearls. Today we are more familiar with Shakespeare's parody than with what it parodies:

> My mistress's eyes are nothing like the sun
> Coral is far more red than her lips' red . . .

Perhaps the key word is *cliché.* The first use of a "used-up" expression is not hackneyed; it is the lack of originality that finally makes the expression objectionable. (Milton was not using a cliché when he wrote *paint the lily,* but all of us who misquote him and say *gild the lily* obviously are.) At any rate, this is what our literature and rhetoric teachers would have us believe. But if hackneyed expressions turn up in Old English poetry, it's all right. They're called kennings then. To call the ocean *the swan road* is to use a kenning, but to refer to Detroit as *the motor city* is cliché. We would not dare to suggest that an American sportswriter should be judged by the same canons of criticism as an Old English poet.

Allusiveness—suggesting a great deal more than is actually said—is one of the strong points of what we call poetic diction. The pleasure that a certain kind of reader finds in the kenning *ring giver of heroes* (meaning 'a king') derives as much from its allusiveness as from anything else. To that reader, it recalls how Germanic leaders of the so-called Heroic Age rewarded their warriors with armbands ("rings") of gold. Whether there is any formal beauty to the phrase, apart from its allusiveness, is questionable. But no quantitative measure would reveal less allusiveness in the horribly mundane "Somebody give me a cheeseburger" (Skeet Miller Band, "Living in the U.S.A."), at least when responded to by a culturally indoctrinated person like a television-raised American teenager. The outsider, who has not internalized the system whereby MacDonald's hamburger chain beats this phrase into the consciousness of millions, will not get the point. But the non-initiate will not find much in *ring giver of heroes* either.

All but the best of us, if we write or talk naturally, are going to use some of the characteristic clusters of words called clichés. Clichés are stale metaphors, our rhetoric teachers tell us. On the other hand, a lot of seemingly plain English words are historically fixed combinations: *daisy* from *day's eye, window* from *wind eye,* to give only the two most familiar ones. Nothing seems as plain and unfigurative as a walrus, but the most elementary student of the English language knows how to derive it from two words virtually equivalent to *whale horse.* To be sure, language historians call these "frozen" rather than stale metaphors. If a metaphor is lucky enough to be frozen early in the history of a language, it may never be accused of being a cliché.

However, with all the British visitors observing and commenting, early American English didn't have the chance that Old English or even Middle English did to freeze its metaphors. Objections were made to them in the very early days, and schoolteachers set about—unsuccessfully—to eliminate them. About the only success the teachers had was in driving such "jargon" out of studies of the history of American English. Linguists who were linguistic relativists were, paradoxically, hypersensitive to the criticism of the schoolteachers they professed to scorn, and they usually tried to pretend they had never heard of the trite expressions the freshman English handbooks condemned.

So here we are, or rather were. The words didn't really show any great difference between American and British English, even when a little bit of data about pronunciation was added. The sentences, on the other hand, were too complex to deal with; they were, as Noam Chomsky and others have demonstrated, at least potentially infinite in number. You can't put an infinite number of items in a dictionary. And you can't deal historically with a comparison between the sets of sentences that, say, an Englishman and an American produce. You can't even prove that they are different, although common sense tells you that they must be. Within such a context, it is impossible to use documentary evidence, as historians have always done. Language history therefore tended to become a matter of pure speculation for a while—great for linguistics, but terrible for history.

The answer to the dilemma lies in precisely the parts of the language the specialists have tried to suppress. If we study our much-maligned jargon and clichés, we will find out something about our language history.

Most rhetoricians object to the "colorless" nature of typically American jargon. *That's the way I put it up* for 'That's the way I construct my theory' was a typical Westernism, according to Albert D. Richardson's *Beyond the Mississippi* (1867), an excellent source for frontier language materials. This is not the stuff of great poetry, and most freshman English handbooks would condemn it; but it is an authenticated Westernism, and as such it has as much interest for the historian of language as a more literary expression. Alfred Holt's *Phrase Origins* (1936) declares that "a cant expression . . . was 'Nantee palaver'—

nantee standing for Italian *niente,* nothing." This expression is not so well documented as *put it up,* and the statement could be regarded as questionable. On the other hand, it has been established that *palaver* was widely used in the West, and its distribution in Pidgin English should make us wary of rejecting Holt's evidence. In view of what so many other observers reported of frontier American usage, the very word *cant* should awaken a certain interest.

Jargon is important to the historian of American English for another, very special reason. Virtually every lingua franca, and certainly every pidgin, has been stigmatized as jargon. Generally, speakers in a multilingual contact situation have to use a language in which they do not have native proficiency; therefore they seldom scale the heights of rhetoric. Everyone calls the contact language used by the Indians of the Northwest *Chinook Jargon,* perhaps because so many people understand it. Pidginists and students of lingua francas have railed against the use of the term jargon. But languages don't need any defense against such attacks. If everyone says there's a connection between pidgins and jargon, there probably is. And if early observers insisted that American English was full of jargon and that the pidgins were jargons, perhaps both statements are true. Furthermore, the early observers may have put their fingers on something basically important about American English and its development.

Pidginisms have remained in strange places in the American vocabulary. Weseen's *Dictionary of American Slang* (1934) calls *no go* 'lack of agreement' general slang, and *no likee* 'poorly received, unsuccessful' theatre slang; both are certainly pidgin in structure. As the various chapters of this book will show, pidgin expressions show up sporadically in the usage (I prefer to avoid the word slang) of cowboys, trappers, and other frontier American groups. One might ask what theatre people have in common with motley groups like Black and Chinese forced-labor units.

There would seem to be only one possible answer—a multilingual environment.

Early observers like Captain Frederick Marryat (see Chapter VI, especially) were struck by the influence of the American's work on his "slang." Any job or profession—from mathematical linguist to automobile mechanic—develops its own terminology, which is virtually unintelligible to those not engaged in the same work, even to native speakers of the same language. In present-day multilingual societies, like the West Cameroon, workers who migrate from their native villages to work on an occupation complex enough to involve a special jargon have to use the contact language—Pidgin English. Something very similar may have been happening (as eyewitnesses suggest) in the multilingual work groups of the American frontier.

To emphasize the effect on American English of trappers, cowboys, and advertising men, along with the French, the Dutch, gamblers, drinkers, smokers, and, of course, Blacks, who interacted with and influenced all these groups throughout the course of American history, is not to say that these were necessarily the most important influences on the language. The British immigrants who came to this country and became farmers and sheepherders obviously made a significant contribution. But this group, which built fences and stayed put for the most part, has been studied almost to death and presented in one book after another, as though it were the only group of any importance. To assert that phrases originating with miners *(pan out, pay dirt, peter out, strike it rich, stake a claim to)* were important to the development of American English is not to say that farmers' terms *(slop bucket/swill pail, whiffletree, hay doodle/stack/cock, roasting ears, lead-horse)* were not. A test of the ability to express metaphorical concepts in other contexts might, however, tend to favor the former group.

When we look at the historical backgrounds of certain

"cant" phrases, we often find data of unexpected interest. Edwin Newman's *Strictly Speaking* (1974) raises objections to the phrase *just for openers*. If we uncover the history of that phrase, we find that it, like many other familiar terms, originated in the Western United States in the nineteenth century and first applied to poker playing. It was then extended metaphorically to other domains. One may still object to the term, but one should be at least a little amused by it.

Newman finds that "business puts pressure on language" and, under that pressure, "compounds abound" (p. 139), but it was not business pressure that produced *for openers*. The cowboy playing poker was having fun. Long before big business came into being in the United States, compounds of this sort were being produced in American English, somewhat more prolifically than in British English. Drinking as well as poker playing was a prime source. Compounds we Americans have always had with us; some of them we got from the Indians (see Chapter 1).

I do not mean to attack Edwin Newman. I am delighted by many of the statements in *Strictly Speaking*, which confirm the historian's feeling that there has been, all along, something *sui generis* about American English. In the following pages, I argue that compounds and fixed phrases (clichés, if you like) are the key to what has been most characteristic of American English, from the colonial period to the present. The study of these compounds and expressions is fascinating. They have been around for as long as two hundred years, and it is unlikely that anyone is going to drive them out of existence.

Most of them came from the frontier and the West. To be sure, a number originated in the Eastern colonies during the period of contact with the Dutch, the Indians, and other foreign language groups, but thereafter the great bulk seem to have come from the West. They move, then, in the opposite direction to the route of the immigrating Englishmen and the pioneers. The usual picture of American English forms is that they moved westward, according to settlement patterns; yet as I undertook my research for this book, the other pattern emerged so strongly that it could not be ignored.

It is true that some poker terms, which originated in New Orleans and went up the Mississippi with the river boatmen, followed the migration. But the majority of such terms developed in the West and were later transmitted to the East. The movement of poker and drinking terms, of terms associated with lumbering, mining, cattle-raising, and many other occupations, was from the frontier to the East—directly against the flow of the major American settlement pattern.

My research also suggests that it is not necessarily true that a dominant population (in this case the Anglo-Saxon colonists) imposes its vocabulary on other populations, at least not in any uncomplicated pattern. Indians influenced American English long after they had lost control of their territories. The major Dutch influence was felt after the colonies of New York and New Jersey had come under the control of the British. French continued to influence usage in Louisiana for more than a century after the state had become officially English-speaking. There were, of course, initial stages (as with the Mexicans in the Southwest) in which the later-subjugated populations achieved equality or even a type of dominance. Again, however, it is necessary to examine each historical stage separately to formulate statements with any degree of accuracy.

AMERICAN
TALK

1

Yankee Doodle's Second Language— Pidgin English

The most obvious and perhaps most overlooked fact about early American English is that the first English colonists in North America had to communicate with members of other groups, at least two of which could not possibly have been English-speaking— Indians and West African slaves. The latter group was present in appreciable numbers in Massachusetts, Connecticut, and New York, as well as in the South, by the second quarter of the seventeenth century. There were also speakers of other European languages—notably Dutch, French, and German. Histories tend either to frustrate us by overlooking the problem of communication between these groups or to tantalize us by stressing the use of interpreters without answering the basic question: How did the Europeans first communicate with the interpreters?

The final answer will not be provided here, but some suggestions as to the direction the investigation might profitably take can be offered. No one can seriously believe that waving arms and other gestures, however useful they might be in such rudimentary matters as indicating willingness to interact in a friendly manner or warning that a nearer approach would mean battle, were the medium of any real communication at the level of exchange of information. Students of body language are aware that gestures themselves are culture-specific and have to be learned through some kind of transmission, in almost the same way that languages are learned. However, at just this period in the world's history, what are called contact languages or lingua francas (for present purposes, it is not necessary to distinguish precisely between the two) were playing a vitally important role.

In the days when large populations moved long distances by sea, it was essential to have a second language. Sabir, the lingua franca of the Mediterranean and of the Levant, where Captain John Smith of Pocahontas fame spent a lot of time just before coming to Virginia, was the most useful of these.[1] Its grammatical structure could be adapted to a wide range of vocabulary variation; perhaps one reason it escaped general academic notice for so long was that lay linguists who observed it were concerned only with vocabulary and therefore took it for a "corrupted" French, Spanish, Italian, Provençal, Catalan, or a combination of two or more of these.

By looking through extensive but little-known documents, dedicated researchers have ferreted out the widespread use of Sabir by Europeans traveling outside Europe.[2] One of the easiest references to find is a statement in the seventeenth-century volume *Hakluytus Post-humus, or Purchas His Pilgrimes* about the "savages" in a part of Canada:

> Whereof the Savages being astonied, did say in words borrowed from the Basques, Endia Chave Normandia, that is to say, that the Normans know many things.[3]

The interpretation of this quotation is a problematic but important one. *Chave* looks like *savvy,* a pidgin vocabulary item that occurs in many varieties of pidgin languages but seems to have come originally from the Portuguese Pidgin that preceded all the others in the world of the European maritime expansion.[4] By default, *endia* must mean 'many things'—since *Normandia* must mean 'Normans'. How the author knew that these words were "borrowed from the Basques," I have no idea. Basques were not very prominent in the European maritime expansion, and it is quite possible that *Normandia* meant something quite different then than it does today. (*Ethiopian,* for example, in texts of the same period, meant any African, especially a West African, the only type Europeans in the New World were ever likely to run into, rather than anyone who had ever lived in the vicinity of Addis Ababa.) On the other hand, *Normans* may be a more correct term, by our standards, than the author thought. He probably meant seagoing Frenchmen, who were stereotypically labeled "Normans."[5] This kind of modification of the lingua franca was going on in coastal areas and on islands all over the world, and "savages" were often involved.

Like most of these "savages," the natives of North America were forced to learn some form of lingua franca, depending upon which European groups they happened to need to cope with.[6] The most interesting for our purposes is Pidgin English, one of the many developments in the Sabir tradition.[7] The American Indians, of course, had their own languages, more or less one per tribe,[8] and the Indian tribes of the East Coast had contact languages, which white men sometimes learned, used, and adapted. We have some studies of the

> curious white man's Indian of the eighteenth century in New Jersey, which was used as a trader's language in much the same way as Chinook Jargon of the present day.[9]

"White man's Indian," although very bad from the point of view of Indian purism, was at least recognizable. Investigator J. Dyneley Prince, a one-time lieutenant governor of New Jersey, concluded that the New Jersey Jargon "was based on Lenape."[10]

Usually, however, the Indians had to learn the white man's language, under far from ideal learning conditions. The British immigrants to Plymouth Rock, who do not seem to have worried very much about the Indians' communication problems, apparently thought that it happened by a kind of magic. William Bradford's *Of Plimouth Plantation,* possibly the first account of the language variety used by Indians in contact with the English, records that

> about the 16th of March [1621], a certain Indian came boldly among them and spoke to them in broken English, which they could well understand but marveled at it.

As it turned out, this Indian had acquired English by a process quite different from magic:

> At length they understood by discourse with him, that he was not of these parts, but belonged to the eastern parts where some English ships came to fish, with whom he was acquainted and . . . amongst whom he had got his language.

The Indian, whose name insofar as the Puritans were able to render it was Samoset, told of another Indian named Squanto (otherwise Tisquantum, which may turn out to be important) "who had been in England and could speak better English than himself." Elsewhere it is recorded that Squanto had learned his English after having been carried away in 1614 by "one Hunt, a mr. [master] of a ship, who thought to sell them for slaves in Spain." He managed to return to Massachusetts in 1618, possessed of a knowledge of English if not much else in compensation for his troubles.

Many other learners of English suffered similar disadvantages in that period. The elements associated with the language were all too often not only the sea and commerce but the slave trade. Native Americans as well as Africans were involved. In Spanish America, a Bishop Las Casas is famous for his "humanitarian" action, in the early sixteenth century, of recommending the importation of West African slaves—"humanitarian" because the Indians were dying off in slavery, and the Africans were able to endure it. The historian of African-Indian relationships in New England, Lorenzo J. Greene, tells how, in the eighteenth century,

> considerable intermixture went on between Negroes and other racial groups, especially between Indians and Negroes. It was said that many Indian slaves in Connecticut lost their social identity by intermarriage with Negroes . . .[11]

Although forced labor was a significant part of the picture, the history of American English is not complete without including maritime use and the spread to native speakers of other languages. The situation must have been somewhat like that described in a nineteenth-century report from another area by one Lieutenant Boteler, second officer to Captain William Fitzwilliam Owen during a voyage on H.M.S. *Leven:*

> The whalers, when employed in fishing in the [Delagoa] Bay are in the habit of hiring the natives for a mere trifle to perform such duties as would expose their own men to the baneful effects of the climate . . . hence it is that the English language is understood and spoken by the Delagoa men, and by some few remarkably well.[12]

Delagoa Bay, off the coast of East Africa, was one of the many maritime areas (Cape Cod was another) where both

English and a variety of Portuguese were in use and where other language groups also contributed to a multilingual pattern.

The case for West African slaves' use of Pidgin English has been made elsewhere.[13] To some degree, even earlier attestations can be made for American Indian Pidgin English. William Wood, an Englishman who published his comments on America in *New England's Prospect* (1634), describes how Indians rowing out to a ship and being fired upon said, "What much hoggery!"—obviously not an expression of pleasure—described the size of the ship by saying, "so big walk," expressed their feelings about the sound of the guns with the words "so big speak," and concluded "by and by [probably the familiar Pidgin English *bimeby*] kill" and beat a retreat. In the land records of Duke's County at Edgartown, Massachusetts, some conveyances, agreements, and other instruments are written by Indians in their own language with some English words phonologically altered by the Indian language pattern. They wrote (and presumably pronounced something like) *ake* for *acre, akinnew* or *akussio* for *acres, noddo* for *rods,* and in one case *nummo* for *rum.* Substitution of *n* for *r* is not unusual in this early contact picture; the most famous case is that of *cannibal* from the same word as *Caribe* and *Caribbean.*[14]

The scene along the streets of Roxbury, Massachusetts, in the 1640's has been described by religious historian Ola Elizabeth Winslow, in her biography of missionary John Eliot, in the following terms:

> Something to sell, something to buy, brief exchange in half-understood Pidgin English or Pidgin Algonquian phrases, not quite friendship, not quite conscious fear on either side; mere acceptance.

Recorded examples of the English pidgin from Massachusetts around 1675 read like

"Umh, umh, me no stawmere fight Engis mon, Engis mon got two hed, Engis man got two hed, if me cut off one hed, he got noder, a put on beder as dis."[15]

Even Douglas Leechman and Robert A. Hall, Jr., pioneers in the study of American Indian Pidgin English, were confused by *stawmere* and suggested (weakly) that it might be from *stomach*. Other attestations, however, make it clear that the word, sometimes spelled *stomany*, means 'understand'.[16] Vocabulary items like *netop* 'friend' were widely current in the Pidgin English of the Massachusetts area and passed into eighteenth-century American English, but have since disappeared. Others like *squaw* and *papoose* were picked up there and carried across the continent by frontiersmen. Still others, like *savvy* and *palaver,* came from the maritime trade, remained in general American Indian Pidgin English, and were transmitted into the English dialects of the American West. Pidgin English was, it appears, more a language in its own right than even professional students have realized.

A missionary journal published in Connecticut in the nineteenth century, *The Religious Intelligencer,* contains, in its 1821 issue, a very long selection entitled "Poor Sarah" in which an Indian woman is represented as a virtually monolingual speaker of a variety of English that has extensive pidgin/creole characteristics:

"Not often, misse; sometimes I get so hungry for it [meat], I begin feel wicked; then think how Jesus hungry in the desert. But when Satan tempt him to sin, to get food, he would not. So I say, Sarah won't sin to get victuals. I no steal, no eat stole food, though be hungry ever so long."

In spite of a great deal of influence from Standard English, the above quotation contains the striking Pidgin English feature of zero copula *(how Jesus hungry)* in a non-present-tense context ('how Jesus was hungry' rather than 'how Jesus is hungry'). Altogether, there are a dozen pages or so of her speech.

Quite early in the British-Indian contact, the burden of communication was already on the Indian, who obviously had to learn Pidgin English if he wanted to go away from his tribe. The white men had whatever comprehension of the Pidgin variety results from knowledge of Standard English, plus the advantage that the Indians would usually accept correction of their "corrupt" language forms. A few white men used the "curious Indian [language]" reported by Prince, but only in very special circumstances. Missionaries like Roger Williams and John Eliot, who learned some form of the Indian language, were a decided minority among the white population. There were, however, things that the Indian knew and the white man needed to learn, especially in the early days. In many cases, the European needed the Indian's word for the object or the technique involved in its use. The Indians' knowledge of Pidgin English made it possible for the white at least to ask, "What dat?"

The word for whatever "dat" might be, like the name of poor Tisquantum, suffered an occasional strange mutation in the process of coming into first Pidgin and then Standard English. The animal we call a *raccoon* was named in a number of different forms by the colonists. John Smith, who first wrote it down in 1608, spelled it *Raughroughouns*. It's hard to tell what Smith, no phonologist, meant to indicate about the pronunciation, but it seems likely that the word was trisyllabic. (Remember that Squanto had three syllables in the Indian version of his name.) By 1610, Virginians were calling them *Aracouns,* which still looks like three syllables. But the Indian syllable structure was somewhat different from that of any variety of English, and the raccoon lost his first syllable.[17]

The same thing happened, apparently, to *scuppernong,*

the first recorded form of which is *askuponong;* to *opossum* (to which nobody in the English-speaking world today ever grants a first syllable); and to *skunk (seganku* or *segongw* in early attestations). *Squash* was first recorded as *isquontersquash* and *squantersquash,* and *chinkapin* as *checkinqumin.* All sorts of Indian words were affected in this way; we could call this pidginization if all our reference books hadn't taught us that "foreigners" pidginize European languages rather than vice versa.

Other processes, like folk etymology or the use of English-sounding elements in compounds *(woodchuck* from something like *otchack* or *atchitamon),* as well as the usual English speaker's trouble with Indian language sounds, helped the process along.

Counting only individual vocabulary contributions from Indian languages, we have a "relatively minor" impact on American English, according to some observers.[18] The conclusion has not been universally accepted, however. The prominent linguist and dialectologist Albert Marckwardt has pointed out:

> By the time all functional changes [*to tomahawk* from the noun *tomahawk, to skunk* from the noun *skunk*] compounds [*pokeweed* and *pokeberry* from *poke; hickory leaf borer, hickory horned devil,* and *hickory gall aphid* from *hickory*], and derivatives [*caucusable, caucusdom,* and *caucusified* from *caucus*] are taken into account, something less than fifty loan words have added many times that number of lexical units to the language. According to one [unidentified] estimate, present-day English contains some 1700 words from the Indian languages.[19]

But once having established the magnitude of the Indian contribution, Professor Marckwardt seems to want to retreat from his own conclusion, adding the modifying statement that the number "does seem incredibly large."

To illustrate how the compounding referred to above works, we might consider the case of *opossum,* a maximally trivial word and animal, one might think, until the days of Pogo. Most of us know that the opossum is a timid animal which, when frightened, goes into a kind of coma. The enemy sometimes assumes it is dead and leaves it alone. The early settlers—or perhaps the Indians—anthropomorphically concluded that the opossum was really clever and deliberately tricked his enemy—"played possum." Early linguistic associations with the opossum stressed this concept of imitation, so that a possum haw is the *Viburnum nudum,* the inedible berries of which resemble the more palatable ones of the black haw *(Viburnum prunifolium).* An opossum mouse is a pygmy species of opossum, an opossum rug is a name for the skin of an Australian species, an opossum shrew is an insectivorous mammal, and an opossum shrimp, a special type of crustacean.

Other phrases including the word *opossum* were probably widely current in America's early period even though they are archaic or completely obsolete today. In Alexander Mackay, Esq.'s *The Western World, or Travels in the United States in 1846-7,* Philadelphia Blacks touting to travelers the hotels for which they work are quoted:

> . . . Barnum's—only house in town—rest all sham—skin but no 'possum . . .

Robert A. Hall, Jr., was struck by the number of noun-noun compounds (e.g., *baby hands*) to be found in the rather limited corpus of pidgin texts examined for the article he and Douglas Leechman wrote on American Indian Pidgin English, the first such study ever made. In fact, he went so far as to consider the possibility of an Indian language "substratum" for American English. He wound up rejecting the possibility because English had had such compounds before contact with the Indian languages, apparently never considering that the increase in the frequency of such forms might very well reflect Indian language influence. British observers have often exclaimed about the number of such compounds in American English (see, especially, Chapter V), and even more are being added in the twentieth century (see Chapter VII).

The crucial issue, however, is the impact of the Indians on colonial life. If their cultural influence was great, then their linguistic influence may have been also. In this connection it is extremely important to keep in mind the "advanced" culture of the Six Nations of the Iroquois. Contact with the Iroquois may never have been as intimate as it was with the West African slaves in the South, where Black "mammies" tended the aristocratic white children and let their own children play with their charges, but the early American colonists had a great deal to learn from the Nations—and their more intelligent representatives knew it.

The Iroquois were not nomads but occupants of well-defined territories. They coexisted in a loosely knit federation with rules for the interaction of different tribes— rules which apparently were pretty well obeyed. They had a constitution that influenced the political philosophy of Benjamin Franklin, George Washington, and other founding fathers of the United States. Many of its principles are said to have been woven into the United States Constitution. But before the Constitution, the founding fathers framed the more loosely organized Articles of Confederation, and a nonhistorian may be permitted to wonder whether that document was not even more strongly influenced by the system of the Nations. It might also be remembered that the Southern states, when they decided to secede, stressed a less federalist organization, which they believed had been the original concept of the United States.

At any rate, it is certain that early white American

political organizations were aware of the Iroquois. In July 1775, the Continental Congress wrote "A Speech to the Six Confederate Nations" with terms borrowed from Indian English:

> This is a family quarrel between us and Old England. You Indians are not concerned in it. We don't want you to take up the hatchet against the King's troops. We desire you to remain at home and not join on either side, but keep the hatchet buried deep.[20]

Take up the hatchet and *bury the hatchet* were obviously translations from Iroquois, and the early settlers had good reason to learn the Indian way of expressing those concepts.

Earlier, when four Indian chiefs had been sent to an audience with Queen Anne in London, Peter Schuyler, the mayor of Albany and the protector of the Mohawk, had provided them with an address in Standard English interspersed with translation phrases from their own language. The chiefs accompanied the presentation of belts of wampum to Anne with the words:

> As a token of our friendship we hung on the kettle and took up the hatchet . . . Messengers crossed the Great Water in great canoes.[21]

Compounds like *great water* and *great canoes* are well attested (see below).

Squanto, the Indian who greeted the Puritans in their first winter, not only spoke Pidgin English to them but also

> showed them how to plant maize and how to "dress and tend" it . . . he instructed them in the technique of using fish for fertilizer. This was a crucial factor in the survival of the colony, for their English seeds did not sprout.[22]

The English colonists of South Carolina had much the same experience and survived only because their West African slaves knew about rice planting.[23] Thus the Indians and the slaves, with whom the Europeans communicated in Pidgin English, were much more important to the survival of the early colonists than has been generally recognized.

Since colonial Englishmen repaid the Indians by enslaving them and taking their women, the two groups were soon at war. Even the fighting, however, contributed something to the colonial character. When the Revolutionary War brought American troops into conflict with the British Redcoats, the Americans had been trained not in the formal tactics of European warfare but in the guerrilla tactics they had learned fighting the Indians. George Washington knew little about the conduct of a formal pitched battle, but he could cope with the wilderness in a way that was entirely foreign to the British.

Fighting doesn't necessarily mean talking, but all the other activities suggest that colonial Americans discoursed with the Indians a great deal:

> Public speaking was developed into a true art form by the Native American people, and their oratorical skills had a considerable impact upon the Anglo-Americans . . . the speeches made by the natives during treaty negotiations aroused much interest and were widely circulated in printed form. Several generations of school children were exposed to the speeches of Logan and other famous chiefs, and oratory in the United States may well have been considerably embellished thereby.[24]

Furthermore, American children, still in the linguistically formative stage and therefore more important to language history than adults, were often closely associated with both Indians and Blacks:

> In the earlier meeting house the interior had been divided, democratically enough, with benches for the men on the right of the pulpit and for the women on the left

with the gallery reserved for the boys of the town,
Negroes and Indians.[25]

Many of the earlier commentators on American history
apparently never noticed the irony of phrases like "dem-
ocratically enough" in the description of a situation in
which Negroes, Indians, and children were banished to
the gallery. Some more ethnically aware historians, like
Jack D. Forbes, are beginning, however, to investigate the
activities and attitudes of our early "democrats." Forbes
quotes with approval the speculation of Smithsonian In-
stitution director Wilcomb F. Washburn about

> the stereotyped representation in literature of the dark
> girl as wild, passionate, and alluring but somehow tainted
> in blood, so that the hero must return to proper, cold,
> respectable blondness[26]

as possibly reflecting something in colonists' early relationship with the Indians. Certainly there is plenty of evidence
of white males finding sexual contacts more easily with
Indian women than with the females of their own groups.
It is common historical knowledge that the corn Squanto
and other Indians taught the Puritans to grow was different from English corn, that the term *maize* was first
adopted from the Indians for the new crop, but eventually
gave way to a semantically shifted *corn* (at first *Indian
corn*). The new type of corn gave rise to all sorts of other
terms. British corn had no cob, so *corncob* (1819)—as in
corncob pipe and *corncob shell*, which was once made by
removing the pith of the cob and filling the hollow with
powder—has to be American. *Cob* might mean 'a small
stack of hay or grain' in some British dialects, but imagine
what the vulgar "Cob you!" (the older and more rural
predecessor of "Up yours!") would mean to a Briton
speaking the English dialect. *Corny,* perhaps the most

familiar term of opprobrium in show business, is author-
itatively derived from *corn-fed,* in spite of some phonological difficulties with the derivation and the competing
possibility of the French *corné* 'vulgar, outdated'.

Corn shucks, cornhusks, corn bread, corn dodgers, and
corn flakes all pertain to American, not European corn.
The British corn laws, a big thing for nineteenth-century
English reform movements, seem absurdly trivial to American undergraduate history students, whereas *grain laws*
might not. *The Dictionary of Americanisms* has eight
pages of *corn* and its compounds, and not a single one
would have the same semantic profile without the different nature of our Indian-derived corn.

Customs associated with corn production prove to have
been strongly influenced by the Indians. Among the
Ojibwas,

> big fields were husked collectively in giant husking bees.
> The Society of the Dog or Fox was notified by the village
> crier that a husking would take place and the young men
> would come looking for their girls, and the fires for the
> feast would be started for the young men had to be fed.
> The shucking went on all day and far into the night.[27]

The importance of the husking bee in frontier life hardly
needs to be pointed out. The religious significance of the
corn dance, associated with the sowing or harvesting of
corn, may not have been transmitted to white men, but
there are attestations of their use of the term between
1836 and 1903.

Foods developed from Indian corn included *corn pone*
(or *Indian pone*) and *hominy.* The latter was associated
with the Negro in the South, although the New Orleans
Picayune for 1840 reported "The homminy is nothin' but
Ingin chop." *Chop,* which suggests the West African
Pidgin English *chop* 'eat' or 'food', appears to mean 'food'

in this context and probably in the doublet compound *chop feed* (1852) and in an 1830 compound in which it is used to refer to cattle feed.

Other plants indigenous to the New World were called by indigenous names. Persimmon, a shortened form of Renape *pasimenan* 'dried fruit', is one of the most widely used terms. The earliest recorded form of the word in English is *putchamins*. Like a lot of other Indian words, it has lost its first syllable and become *'simmon* in rural colloquial American. Children lucky enough to live where it grows know how delicious it tastes when ripe, and the consequences of eating it when it is not. It is often said down South that a sour-faced person "looks like he's been eatin' a green 'simmon." Captain John Smith's early account of Virginia gives us the first—possibly exaggerated—report in English of such eating; Smith found the experience absolute torture.

The huckleberry, on the other hand, got a "corrupted" form of a name that had been around in English for a long time and was merely applied to the American plant as a special development in American English. According to *The Oxford English Dictionary*, the name is "conjectured to be a corruption of *hurtleberry, whortleberry*." This isn't the kind of explanation etymologists like, but apparently no one has come up with a better one. Derivation from *hurtleberry* is possible within the American context (assuming a non-*r* pronouncing dialect), since "deeper" Creole varieties of Black English replace medial *t* with *k (likkle* for *little, turkle* for *turtle)*. Derivation from *whortleberry,* on the other hand, would lead us into outright mysticism.

From whatever diverse backgrounds, the Indian persimmon and the English (with maybe a touch of Creole) huckleberry soon got together in American proverbial lore. The first recorded quotation, from 1833, tells how the speaker "wouldn't risk a huckleberry to a persimmon."

Since the Nipissing cognate *pasiminan* means 'a raisin or dried huckleberry', the expression—meaning that objects of little value are involved—appears to reflect the frontiersman's knowledge of Indian languages and their terms for native fruits.

Another proverbial expression, "just a huckleberry over my persimmon," is first attested in the work of Davy Crockett. He didn't necessarily originate it, however. It may have been taken over from the Indians by Blacks, since Florida Negroes in Zora Neal Hurston's *Mule and Men* were using it in the 1930's and *'simmon beer* was drunk by plantation slaves in the nineteenth century according to many reports.

Persimmon alone appeared in a large number of other proverbial expressions: *to rake the persimmons* 'to take in the spoils', *to knock down the persimmons* 'to have success', and *that's persimmon* or *all persimmon* 'that's fine'.

American frontiersmen carried not only the Algonquian proverbial usage of huckleberries but also their own versions of other Algonquian words far beyond the territory of the Nations. Words like papoose and squaw—the latter of which was particularly objectionable to the Plains Indians and known to them as a "white man's word"—traveled all the way to the Pacific Coast. McCulloch's *Woods Words,* a dictionary of the special usages of the lumbermen of the Northwest, contains several compounds with *squaw.* The agent of transmission was obviously Pidgin English rather than the Indian languages per se. This contact language—and other contact languages like the Chinook Jargon of the Pacific Northwest—easily took in words from other European languages as well as from Indian languages. *Calumet,* a very early term for 'peace pipe', looks much more Indian in print than *caucus;* but actually it is Romance (Norman French *chalumet,* ultimately from Latin calamus 'reed'), while *caucus* is pure

Algonquian despite its apparent nominative-singular Latin affix. *Siwash,* the Chinook Jargon word for 'Indian', which became the slang term for the American university ("I'd die for dear old Siwash"), is from the French *sauvage.*

The fact that these terms were not originally Amerindian in the strictest etymological sense does not lessen the Indian influence. As primary users of Pidgin English, not only with Englishmen but with the new tribes with whom they were forced into contact as the white man pushed them West, the Indians controlled the important process of compound formation. *Fire* is Germanic enough for anyone, but it was also a favorite combining element in American Indian Pidgin English. Neither *firewater* nor its early synonym *fire drink* is Germanic, even if the two words composing it are. A *fire* could also come to mean a household, family, or nation, so that by 1775 whites could write of *people of one fire* in describing a tribal or political group. *Fire cakes* were browned over the open fire. A *fire hunt,* which the Europeans learned from the Indians, was a way of driving game into the open by setting the underbrush on fire. In 1800, an American reported that the Indians were having a *fire dance* every night in order to bring back to life their *fire maker*—the one who 'makes the fire as early in the morning as he can'. An important man in the tribe was described as the *fire keeper,* in principle a compound not too different from Old English *hlaf weard* 'loaf keeper' (the source of *lord*), except that constant use by the community of native speakers reduced the latter to one semantically obscure syllable whereas the former retained its original form and transparent origin.

Some of the Pidgin compounds are obsolete by now, but speakers of English knew and used them in the early period when American English was getting its stamp of individuality. It isn't quite certain whether *fireworks,* for example, came from the same *fire* tradition or not, but the first attestation is in the "ignited arrow" tradition, which is known to have been part of Indian warfare. In this case, as in the others, the term, once adopted by the white community, underwent significant semantic changes.

The words *big* and *great* entered even more Indian English compounds than *fire*. Aside from the examples already cited, there are expressions as well known as *great spirit* and *big chief*. (The latter varied with *sachem* in Algonquian English contexts, the white men showing off their knowledge of Indian words by insisting upon the use of *sachem* and the Indians passing as speakers of English by using *big chief*.) *Great white father*, by now impossibly hackneyed, is well attested in the early period. *The Dictionary of Americanisms* recognizes *big canoe, big dog, big heart, big lodge, big medicine, big river, big speak, big talk, big village,* and *big water*.

Nobody seems very sure of the origin of all these *big* terms. *The Dictionary of Americanisms,* which is very diffident about such matters, states simply that they appear "in Indian talk or with reference to Indian usage"; elsewhere, it uses "in imitation thereof." Neither *The Dictionary of Americanisms* nor *The Oxford English Dictionary* can make up its mind whether these are loan translations from Algonquian or other Indian languages, carry-overs of something British but not attested elsewhere, or spontaneous improvisations (like getting an especially strong drink of firewater and screaming "Big fire!").

It might, however, be noted that the West African slaves (who were in very close contact with the Indians) spoke a Pidgin English that in all probability made use of *big* in analogous or even identical compounds. Schneider's *Wes-Kos Glossary* of modern Cameroonian Pidgin English lists thirty-one compounds of this type, omitting *big day* 'holiday' which I know from personal experience to have been used in the East Cameroon. Nineteenth-century Western traveler Albert D. Richardson observed of American Indian usage, "Here are their literal renderings of a few common words—*Sunday—the big day.*"[28]

Everyone knows Theodore Roosevelt's *big stick* proverb, but too few have bothered to look up the original quotation: "I have always been fond of the West African proverb 'Speak softly and carry a big stick; you will go far'." *Big mouth* 'excessive talk, loquacity' is an Americanism; so is *too big for one's breeches* 'having an excessive notion of one's own importance', first attested in the writings of Davy Crockett.

Early commentators felt that Indian influence on colonial English was great. The American periodical modeled on the British *Lounger, The Port Folio* "by Oliver Old-school, Esq." for August 1, 1801, objects that a certain Americanism "can be found in no *English* author. It is undoubtedly the growth of the wigwam, and is a vicious scoundrel, and true American word." It does not matter whether the specific form the author is so excited about, *lengthy,* is really of such origin or not. The point is that this early observer thought of some Americanisms as being what he called "wigwam words," which he enjoined Englishmen against using.

The word *Yankee* is one of the etymological puzzles of the colonial period and may even be a "wigwam word." In *All-American English* I showed that the popular solution, that it is a "mispronunciation" of the word *English* by the Indians, has just as much chance of being accurate as any of the supposedly superior suggestions. (Indian pronunciations like *Yengesee* are represented in sources like James Fenimore Cooper's *The Deerslayer,* and Cooper is a rather good source for American Indian Pidgin English.) The rejection of this etymology has been based on the absurd notion that the Indians, having their own word(s) for *Englishman,* would never need to use the English word, which implies that the English and the

Indians (not to mention the French, whose *Anglais* might have contributed something to the vowel quality) had never been in any language contact situation! As I pointed out, the *-ee* ending could be the enclitic vowel of Pidgin English, which was actually present in the Chinese Pidgin English word derived from English and is a common feature in all pidgins.

There is still another generally rejected suggestion, the Cherokee *eankee* (which is not a flattering word, meaning something like 'coward'). It isn't very likely as a source, but at least it helps to make the point that there were a lot of languages around in the colonial period. There is also a record of *Yankee* as a name for a Negro slave in South Carolina in 1725. And the anthropologist Melville J. Herskovits has pointed out that Yanki is the name of one of the spirits worshipped in Surinam.[29]

In the colonial period, the most striking use of the term was the song "Yankee Doodle," almost certainly a British soldier's way of ridiculing the nonregulation Rebel troops for their lack of military impressiveness on the parade ground. The first verse is even more puzzling than the etymology of *Yankee:*

> Yankee Doodle went to town
> Riding on a pony.
> He stuck a feather in his hat
> And called it macaroni.

The last word seems so strange that some Americans sing *matrimony* at that point. Few of us, however, see any more sense in that wording.

The accepted solution is that *macaroni* (the name for the pasta dish, all right, but also a symbol of things Italian) was used in England in the eighteenth century to mean a fop—an Italianate dresser. Sticking a feather in his hat would then be Yankee Doodle's way of being fancy and European, showing what a real bumpkin he was.

Maybe—but there's reason to suspect something else, in the beginning at least. A children's play song from Surinam, on the coast of South America, goes

> Mama Nanni go to town
> Buy a little pony.
> Stick a feather in a ring,
> Calling Masra Ranni.
>> Ink, pink, rotten beaf,
>> Toss!

In the next chapter, we will reexamine the linguistic consequences of the fact that Dutch and English (including Pidgin English) coexisted in the colonies of New York and New Jersey, as Dutch and Creole English (a descendant of that Pidgin English) still do in Surinam. We have a ready explanation of the transmission in the exchange of British territory (Surinam) for Dutch territory (New Amsterdam) between 1664 and 1667. We know that colonial children associated with Indians and Negroes far more closely than their parents did, and we know that children are likely to be the ones to pick up a variety of languages in a multilingual context. Add to that the fact that children often hold on to traditional and archaic material in their rhymes and play songs, and there is good reason for suspecting that there may be some connection.

Was Masra Ranni (the first word is the Surinam version of the ubiquitous *Massa* of slavery) the original form? It's at least plausible. The British soldiers may have heard the children's song, thought it ridiculous and therefore a good thing to mock the upstart Americans with, and taken it into their repertory. They obviously added a lot of stanzas, as did the Americans after it became a patriotic symbol. Everybody added stanzas, and there are supposed to be hundreds of them in all the versions. The phonological similarity of *Masra Ranni* and *macaroni* may have impressed some British officer of aristocratic background who was familiar with the world of fashion and saw the satirical possibilities in comparing the ill-dressed American troops to Italianate fops. The explanation that has *macaroni* meaning 'fop' wouldn't then be inaccurate—it would simply not be the explanation for the original stage. The semantics of *fop* perhaps helped to generate the now-familiar refrain "Yankee Doodle dandy." Since George M. Cohan wrote it into his derivative song of blatantly commercial patriotism, and his story was widely disseminated by the movies, most Americans have assumed that it is the one indispensable part of the song.

There is at least one other bit of circumstantial evidence not known to earlier students. In the late eighteenth century, an English broadside entitled "Yankee Doodle, or the Negroes Farewell to America" appeared.[30] It is in a rather artificial form of "Negro English" (one line reads: "Or will me come hither or thither me go/No help make you rich by de sweat of my brow"). Set in the colonial period, it precedes the supposed travesty of Revolutionary American soldiers composed by a British officer.

Be that as it may, Yankee Doodle—his song or his speech—can't be explained apart from the multilingual situation. A word from Italian isn't absolutely necessary, perhaps; but English, French, Dutch, and a variety of Indian languages are. (For the function of Dutch, see the next chapter.) And the thing that linked them all was the contact language, Pidgin English.

2

Yankee Doodle
As Part Dutch

In the maritime trade, which was so vitally important
to early American English, a Dutch sailor was sometimes known as Janke, Little John. (This is a much
more likely source of *Yankee* than Mencken's favorite,
Jan Kees, a kind of Dutch John Doe, with *Kees* misan-
alyzed as a plural and a new singular *Kee* produced.) But
it is unimportant whether the actual word *Yankee* is of
Dutch origin. What is interesting and significant is that
the environment in which the word took on its full set of
associations was subject to influence from, among other
languages, Dutch.[1]

After the British "traded" Surinam to the Dutch in
1667 in return for New York, English Creole continued
to be spoken in Surinam and Dutch Creole in New York.
The Dutch language was often heard in colonies we now
think of as having been English, and the English tongue
was extremely familiar in Dutch areas.

The English and the Dutch were closely associated in
the minds of much of the world in the seventeenth century.
In the collection of sixteenth-century sailing narratives
published under the title of *Purchase His Pilgrimes,* we
can read:

we may reckon those Englishmen in diverse of those Dutch
voyages about the globe, Timothy Shotten, Thomas

Spring, John Caldwell, and others. Yea, the name of Englishman were [sic] so famous in the East, that the Hollanders in their first trade thither, varnished their obscurities with English luster and gave out themselves English.

Dutch use of a song with the same tune as "Yankee Doodle" has been established, albeit for a much later date, and there are even some Dutch words:

> Yanker didel doodel down
> Didel, dudel lanter
> Yanke viver, voover vown
> Botermilk and Tanther.[2]

The stanza is nonsense, and the last line isn't even clear Dutch nonsense (as, for example, "Jabberwocky" is clearly English nonsense) but is in a kind of composite language, like the Surinam "Masra Ranni" rhyme. Transmission of the rhyme and the tune from Surinam to Holland is a definite possibility if the stanza was indeed originally in the Pidgin English used as a contact language between Indians and African slaves in areas of the New World colonized by the English as well as the Dutch.

The first record of the song in Holland is in the nineteenth century, when it was sung by migratory workers. This makes it seem more likely that the Dutch picked it up in the New York–Surinam trade with the English than that they invented it and brought it to the American colonies. By the nineteenth century, the Dutch had been strongly influenced by the English, while influences in the other direction had become rather slight. The chances are that the Dutch use is far from the origin of the song, which I believe originated with African slaves and spread from the Blacks to both the English in New York and the Dutch in Surinam.

What we think of as colonial Yankee characteristics, however, have a great deal in common with the stereotype of the Dutch. Both have a reputation for sharp dealing and frugality, as in the expressions *a Dutch treat* and *to go Dutch*. The rural trader, the earliest of the "Yankee" types, had many of the same traits; *a Yankee trick* was the colonial term for a sharp bargain. And, although it doesn't seem to be in any of the dictionaries, there is also the familiar American expression typifying frugality, *a Yankee dime*. During the Depression, it meant a kiss; asked for money, one could offer "a Yankee dime."

In the domain of money, *dollar* is a good example of Dutch influence on American English. The Dutch and Low German *daler* meant 'coined in the valley', being cognate with the High German *thaler*, which has the same meaning. The word in its present form was common in English before 1600 but did not designate a major unit of British currency. When, about the time of the Revolution, the founding fathers decided to show their independence from England by turning away from pounds and shillings, they decided upon *dollar* as their unit of currency. Its value, however, was pegged most nearly to the "piece of eight" familiar on the Spanish main. Each eighth was worth twelve and a half cents—a *bit*—and terms like *four bits* and *six bits* were used well into the twentieth century. The word, also current in the West Indies in the seventeenth and eighteenth centuries, designated the British or American equivalent of a small Spanish coin; in nineteenth-century America, the specific coin to which the value of the American bit was pegged was the Mexican *real*. In coinage as in other domains, Dutch influence on American usage was closely linked to influences from other languages.

The most important port for international contacts, New York, was first Nieuw Amsterdam, and primacy is important in a language contact situation. The city's most famous street would not necessarily have been named Broadway if the Dutch hadn't called it Bredeweg 'wide road'. The Americans either anglicized or translated Dutch names; in this case, both processes yielded approximately the same result. Flushing, originally Vlissingen, had been named for a port in Holland. Brooklyn, at first Breuckelen, meant 'marshland' in Dutch. The city's professional basketball players would certainly not be the Knickerbockers (an old name for the Hollanders) if the history had been different. Dozens of place names known primarily to residents of New York (like Hell Gate, a rather sloppy rendering of Helle-Gat, and Wallabout, Waale Bobbt) came from Dutch. Harlem, the symbol of Black identity to a great part of the world, was originally Haarlem.

The Dutch were also the first Europeans to settle the land farther up the Tappan Zee, which later became the Hudson River. In Beverwyck (now Albany) they established not only the fur trade but also a pattern of relationship with the local Indians that was to endure for many years. Beverwyck means 'beaver town'. The Dutch were the first to make the beaver (in their language, *bever*) so commercially important that the skins became a medium of currency. Some salaries in the early days were paid in so many "bevers." When the English settlers picked up the usage, they carried it all the way to Oregon. (See Chapter 6 for the importance of the term in the lives of the mountain men.)

The Dutch had more effective relationships with the Indians than the English, and Indian influence remained strong in territory the latter took over from Holland. *Indian posts,* for example, carried the mail to Albany in the winter of 1672. And it was because of established Dutch patterns that one of the first intercontinental conventions, which met in Albany in 1689, included delegates from the Iroquois Confederation as well as from the Massachusetts Bay, Plymouth, Connecticut, and New York colonies. Whenever Indian influence on frontier terminology is suggested in later chapters, it could be argued that it reflects an indirect Dutch influence.

Dutch was widely used in both New York and New Jersey in the seventeenth century. Many observers reported Dutch linguistic and cultural influences in the Hudson Valley, and as late as 1750 a Swedish naturalist named Peter Kahn found that although the dress in Albany was English, the town's language and manners were Dutch.

The most significant reports on the language situation come from a Boston physician named Alexander Hamilton, whose *Itinerarium* of 1744 describes a visit to Albany. Over and over again he comments on the use of Dutch. Approaching the city, he found

> The devil a word but Dutch was bandied about . . . and in general there was such a medley of Dutch and English as would have tired a horse.[3]

In Albany itself,

> one's ears [were] perpetually invaded and molested with volleys of rough-sounding Dutch, which is the language most in use here.

Hamilton makes it clear that it was the Dutch population's insistence on using its own language that produced this regrettable situation. Most Americans, like Hamilton himself, had little use for any foreign languages. The gradual extinction of Dutch in New York—and of French in some parts of Louisiana—was the result of this domineering attitude on the part of the English speakers. A political leader like John Adams, on the other hand, was not above showing off his speaking knowledge of Dutch at dinner parties.[4]

Like many another master in the colonies, Dr. Hamilton depended upon his Black slave when the linguistic going got rough. The servant, named Dromo, was as unhappy with the language situation as Hamilton himself but was more assiduous in coping with it:

> Dromo, being about twenty paces before us, stopped at a house, where, when I came up, I found him discoursing with a negroe girl, who spoke Dutch to him. "Dis de way to York?" says Dromo. "Yaw, dat is Yarikee," said the wench, pointing to the steeples. "What devil you say?" replies Dromo. "Yaw, mynheer," said the wench. "Damne you, what you say?" said Dromo again. "Yaw, yaw," said the girl. "You a damn black bitch," said Dromo, and so rid on.[5]

Despite Hamilton's designation of the girl's language as "Dutch," what she actually spoke seems to have been a mixture of English (the copula form *is,* connecting *dat* and *Yarikee*), Pidgin English (*Yarikee*, with two enclitic vowels, for *York*), and Dutch *(Yaw, mynheer)*. Between them, the English and the Dutch bequeathed similar variations in parts of the world like Surinam, where an English-based Creole (Sranan Tongo) has hundreds of loan words from Dutch.[6]

Such mixing seems to have been very common in the colony of New York. L. G. van Loon, the historian, who is one of the few writers on the subject, reports:

> Some speakers of Hudson-Mohawk Dutch really knew so little "Dutch" that they spoke a jargon of mispronounced American with a hybrid syntax and no more than a fair sprinkling of words of a real Dutch origin, with the result that such expressions as "Weet you dat joe was where je

gheen business had?" — "Do you know that you were
where you had no business?" were fairly common.[7]

But although the Dutch language forms were gradually
worn away, the English of many speakers of the area was
still strongly influenced in subtle ways (see below).

In the area where a contact variety of Dutch coexisted
with Pidgin English, a radically nonstandard variety of
English was fostered. Important historical figures are involved in the language shift from a kind of Dutch to nonstandard English. For example, the famous Black feminist
of the pre–Civil War period, Sojourner Truth, belonged
to a Dutch master in upstate New York until she was
twenty and spoke only Dutch in her early years. Harriet
Beecher Stowe's 1863 *Atlantic Monthly* interview with
her, quaintly entitled "Sojourner Truth: The Libyan
Sibyl," quotes her in Black English. Probably Sojourner
Truth learned that variety after she was freed, and she
made excellent use of it as an inspired public speaker.[8]
Other transcribers of the speech of the great Black sup-
porter of Negro and women's rights corroborate Mrs.
Stowe's evidence. The following is part of the record
made by Frances D. Gage, chairwoman of a women's rights
convention in Akron, Ohio, in May, 1851:

"Wall, chilern, whar dar is so much racket dar must be
somethin' out of kilter. I tink dat 'twixt de niggers of de
Souf and de women at de Norf, all talkin' 'bout rights,
de white men will be in a fix pretty soon. But what's all
dis here talkin' 'bout?

"Dat man ober dar say dat womin needs to be helped
into carriages, and lifted ober ditches, and to hab de best
place everywhar. Nobody eber helps me into carriages,
or ober mud-puddles, or gibs me any best places! An a'n't
I a woman? Look at me! Look at my arm! . . . Den dat

little man in black dar, he say women can't have as much
rights as men, 'cause Christ wasn't a woman! Whar did
Christ come from? . . . Whar did your Christ come from?
From God and a woman! Man had nothin' to do wid
Him."[9]

Sojourner Truth's English clearly belongs in the Black
tradition. We have no such attestations of her Dutch, but
the speech of other slaves belonging to Hollanders in the
area belongs to the Dutch Creole tradition. She and less
famous speakers were using contact varieties of different
European languages at the time that additions to the
American English vocabulary from those languages were
taking place. Her achievement in becoming a prominent
speaker is all the more remarkable in the light of her
linguistic background.

In his 1910 article entitled "Jersey Dutch," J. Dyneley
Prince examined the speech of a number of informants
in the New York area. Prince reported:

> Up to thirty years ago [1880] this was the common idiom
> of many rural districts in northern New Jersey, employed
> alike by Dutch, English, German, and French settlers. It
> has, during the past three decades, been driven from its
> former territory by the public schools, and now survives
> only in the memories of some two hundred old persons,
> nearly all of whom are over seventy years old.[10]

Among Prince's informants was a Black man named
William DeFreece who was part Minsi Indian and described by Prince as "an excellent authority on the negro
variant of the dialect." Prince, who had researcher's skill
enough to cross-check his impressions, found that other
informants "characterized many of his words as distinctly
'nigger'." Prince saw in this survival evidence that "the
negro slaves of the old settlers used an idiom tinged with

their own peculiarities." A less formal earlier writer, Gertrude Leffert Vanderbilt, had asserted approximately the same thing in 1881 when she pointed out that

> the colored people in the kitchen, the master and mistress in the house, neighbor to neighbor and friend to friend, all conversed in Dutch.[11]

She added:

> For a long time, in this mingling of languages, neither of them was grammatically spoken; bad English and worse Dutch was the result . . .[12]

The formal linguist may deprecate her phrase "worse Dutch," but it is an excellent indication of which language was giving way to the other. Corroborating her statement about "colored people . . . master and mistress," Prince observed:

> There is a small colony of old Negroes living on the mountain back of Suffern, N.Y., who still use their own dialect of Jersey Dutch, but they are very difficult of access, owing to their shyness of strangers.[13]

From other sources, we learn that these "old Negroes" came from a settlement of "mixed blood Indians, Negroes, and whites."[14]

The few forms cited by Prince from his Black informant's speech are consistent with the thesis that the "Negro" dialect of Jersey Dutch was a variety of Dutch Creole. The elderly informant used a "present tense" form of a verb in a "past tense" context, which is certainly one of the superficial marks of a creole language. Prince reported that DeFreece "knew no past tense at all"—the kind of remark an investigator who is unwittingly dealing with a creole language often makes. The old man also used the English *when* for the Dutch subordinate time conjunction *wäner* and indulged in "the most curious negroism" in the form of *plôt* 'foot' rather than the Standard Dutch form *pôt*. This insertion of *l* may, however, have been hypercorrection: Creole speakers tend to "leave out" (or vocalize) the liquid consonants *l* and *r*, and when they become aware of this they try to insert the sounds when talking to strangers—sometimes inserting too many. If Joe Frazier actually said, "He don't phrase [that is, *faze*] me" before his first fight with Muhammad Ali,[15] he was engaging in the same process. (See Chapter 4 for a report of this process in the Pidgin English of a Chinese speaker.)

Creole Dutch, which may well have had its origin in the superimposing of Dutch vocabulary on a Pidgin English base,[16] was spoken for many years in the Virgin Islands, and there are still a few elderly informants on the island of St. John who use the language.[17] The thirteen original colonies of the United States had much more in common linguistically with the West Indies than has usually been recognized.

Van Loon gives us additional evidence of the use of a contact variety of Dutch:

> Both the Mohawk-Hudson Dutch and the Jersey dialect sounds were an evolutionary process starting with the earliest colonists who were a Dutch citizenry composed of Hollanders, Frisians, Germans, Irish, English, French, Negroes, and of course the omnipresent Indian.[18]

Black speakers were an important element in this picture. The Dutch brought African slaves to the American mainland as early as anyone else, and they had great numbers of them by 1625 or 1626.

Perhaps the most obvious Black-influenced American-English borrowing is *boss,* from Dutch *baas.* Southern

Black English (and some white dialects influenced by it) have *bossman* as an elaboration on *boss,* 'master foreman', and the word has a wider range of meanings in Black English today than in ordinary English. Black speakers also use it to mean 'excellent, superior' (as in Boss Bat, the name a Washington, D.C., Black gave to his new car in 1967). The word is used in that meaning in the English Creole of Surinam, which is not surprising, since at the time of the exchange of Nieuw Amsterdam for Surinam, between 1664 and 1667, many Black slaves were shipped from one of those areas to the other. Surinam, which has three different English-based Creoles today, still manifests the same kind of linguistic situation that existed in colonial New York. In Afrikaans, the Dutch-based Creole of South Africa, *baas* has the same meaning as in general American English.

Compounds, which are the very essence of the difference between American English and British English,[19] were strongly influenced by the contact with Dutch. Americans turned Dutch *hoi-berg* 'mountain of hay' into *hay barrack,* the Hudson Valley and East Jersey term for what most of the rest of us call *haystack.* Etymologists generally recognize that the American *storm door* did not develop spontaneously but rather was modeled on Dutch *storm deur.* The same kind of influence produced *horse thief,* modeled on Dutch *paardendief.* First attested on the East Coast in 1768, the phrase traveled West to become the designation of the greatest of criminals among the cowboys. *Pot cheese,* a local variant for *cottage cheese,* is a direct adaptation of Dutch *pot keese*—in fact, little more than a few recent developments in the phonology of English distinguishes the two expressions. *Hot cake,* an alternate to older English *pancake,* reflects Dutch *heetekoek.* Even an American vernacular phrase like interrogative *How come?* 'Why?' is from Dutch *hoekom.* It is necessary to remember that a contact variety of Dutch is involved rather than Standard Dutch. The latter was *waarom* (compare the German *warum*). Many, however, of the nonstandard Dutch varieties that reflect multilingual contact situations have *hoekom*.

Individual words derived from Dutch and first attested in American English include *bowery,* from the word originally meaning 'farm' that designated the country lane which later became Manhattan's version of skid row. *Poppycock,* from Dutch *papekak* 'soft dung', is treated today as a euphemism virtually equivalent to "Nonsense!" although historically it was closer to the expletive "Shit!" Interestingly, the first attestation (1865) is an allusion to the speeches of congressmen. Both *cookie* (Dutch *koekje* 'little cake') and *cruller* (Dutch *krulle* 'a crooked piece of pastry') reflect Dutch influence on American cooking. *Olicook,* still used by a few elderly residents of the Hudson Valley, comes from Dutch *olykoek* 'a kind of dough cake fried in fat, or doughnut'. Dutch *log* 'heavy, dull' gave us *logy,* the way an announcer in a television commercial promises we will no longer feel when we take a popular alkalizer. *Dumb,* in the sense 'stupid' rather than 'mute', may be from either Dutch or German—most likely it reflects their combined influences. *Patroon,* the Dutch term applied to the members of the West India Company who were granted manorial privileges in 1758, survived in American English in the more general sense of 'a possessor of a landed estate'. *Stoop* (Dutch *stoep* 'a small porch with seats or benches') was originally a raised, uncovered platform before the entrance of a house but is now used in various parts of the United States for *porch* or *veranda.* Dutch *pit,* etymologically related to English *pith,* is used for the hard stone of the cherry, peach, or plum that contains the seed. Dutch *wafel* became our *waffle,* 'a batter cake baked on a waffle iron'; the word is distantly related to *wafer,* in use in English from medieval times and retained in American English in a meaning quite different from *waffle*. *Scow, sleigh, snoop, span* (of horses), and *spook* were American borrowings from Dutch that have since spread to British English.

The way in which the British *Father Christmas* has been replaced by the American *Santa Claus* is an outstanding example of the multilingual context in which Dutch loan words became a part of American English. Along with its more formal synonym, St. Nicholas, it came from Dutch *Sinter Klaas* in 1773. This St. Nicholas, whose devotees originally gave each other gifts on December 6, had been absorbed into Christmas celebrations in Europe during the Middle Ages and his day changed to December 25. The Dutch did not associate the Christmas tree with him, however; the Germans brought that in, around 1830. They also brought us their name for the new-born Savior, *Christkindlein* or *Christkind'l,* from which Americans made *Kriss Kringle*. Of course, it is possible for Santa Claus to come on Noël—the French term for Christmas; and in bilingual Puerto Rico, Santa Claus comes on Navidad.

In jocular American usage, *plug* means 'a slow horse'. The Dutch *ploeg paard* 'plow horse' is the most likely source. First attested in American English in 1860, it was part of general colonial slang and traveled to Australia and New Zealand during the nineteenth century.

What we call a *saw horse* was not regarded as equine at all by the Dutch, who called it *Zaagbock* 'support for a saw'. First recorded in 1860, our borrowing, *sawbuck* (which could just as easily have come from German *Sägebock*), meant 'a frame for two pieces of wood being cross-cut'. The later meaning 'a ten-dollar bill' appears to have come from the X-shape of the frame, which resembles the Roman numeral for ten. The relationship to *buck,* as in the roughly synonymous *ten bucks,* attested from 1896, is considered obscure by authorities on etymology but undoubtedly helped produce the situation in which a "double sawbuck" could mean twenty dollars. Some mixing between the Dutch/German word and *buck* as used with the poker ante in the West (see Chapter 4) seems to be involved.

The English colonists brought a number of Dutch loan words to the New World, and some of them remain important in our vocabulary:

pickle	freebooter
sled	wagon
spool	isinglass
deck	luck
hoist	spatter
hold (of a ship)	frolic
bulwark	loiter

Some of them—especially those with maritime associations—represent a generalized Low German Lingua Franca of the maritime trade, closely related to the Dutch Creole referred to above rather than to Standard Dutch. *Deck* and *hold* are, obviously, widely used in nonmaritime contexts. In fact, Joanna Carver Colcord *(Sea Language Comes Ashore)* has pointed out that many phrases in which the pronunciation is now more usually "hole" really derive from maritime *hold.* The baseball player who is third in turn at bat is *in the hole*—probably from *hold,* since the second in order is *on deck.*

Boom, borrowed from Dutch in the American colonies, is another reflection of the associations between Dutch borrowings and maritime activity. The word for 'tree' (cf. German *Baum,* Old English *beam*), it was applied in Dutch to the studding (i.e., auxiliary) sails of a ship. Before coming into American English, it had spread into the Mediterranean Lingua Franca (see Chapter 1); it appears in Portuguese as *bome* and in Italian as *boma.* In nautical parlance, the ship with its sails "boomed out" was really "booming along"; the word acquired its optimistic connotation early. In the American West, the verb *boom,* used of a river to mean 'rush strongly', acquired the figurative meaning that makes it the opposite of *bust* in popular economic terminology. (See Chapter 7.)

Another maritime word to acquire figurative meanings on land was Dutch *vrijbuiter* 'one who goes in search of plunder, a pirate', from which we got *freebooter.* Because of the importance of Dutch shipping, it entered English and was transmitted to the maritime vocabularies of other nations, like Spain. Any conventional treatment of American English will tell you that the Americans later borrowed the Spanish version of the same word, *filibuster,* and will go on to explain how a congressman speaking too long before the House was accused of "filibustering" the nation's time (that is, stealing or pirating it) and a new term for legislative activity was born.

There is, however, some trouble with this neatly laid out pattern. For the Dutch *vrijbuiter* to change into the Spanish *filibustero,* some rather extreme changes would have to take place. The initial *fr-* consonant cluster would have to be broken up by the introduction of a vowel and the *r* changed to *l.* Such a result may come about if a cluster like *fr-* is difficult to speakers of a given language. (Consider the case of an uneducated English speaker trying to pronounce the *pn-* in *pneumonia* and coming out with *pee-neumonia.*) Spanish speakers have trouble with English *st-, str-, sp-, spr-, sk-,* and *skr-* in initial position and characteristically insert a vowel before the cluster. But Spanish has no such trouble with *fr-,* since it is full of words with just that cluster in initial position: *franco, frase; fregar, frecuente; friar, fricar; frontera, frotar; fruta, fruncir.* Corominas's *Breve Diccionario Etimológico de la Lengua Española* suggests a Dutch form beginning with *fl-* rather than *fr-,* but the same objection holds. Spanish has *flauta, flexible, flictena, flojo, fluir,* etc. *The Oxford*

English Dictionary has a long discussion of the phonological problem, but comes to no conclusion.

Again, the language variety in which such a phonological change would be most likely to take place would be a pidgin language, one of the type that was most prominent in the nautical language contact situation of colonial times. Typically, such a pidgin breaks up almost all consonant clusters, rendering the pattern easy to pronounce for speakers of any language, no matter what its patterns. Among other things, such a Pidgin Dutch would be the ancestor of the Creole Dutch in use in the Virgin Islands and in colonial New York/New Jersey, and would decreolize into the nonstandard Dutch that Prince and others found in the area, notably among Black speakers, in the early twentieth century.

More standard Dutch provides American place name elements like *kill* 'creek', *dorp* 'village', and *clove* 'valley'. Earlier borrowings, presumably obsolete by now, included *fly* 'a swamp', *overslaugh* 'a sand bar', *fetticus* 'a salad', *blickey* 'a small bucket', *pinxter* 'Whitsuntide' (borrowed by Black slaves on Long Island in the eighteenth century and applied to festivals of their own which were as much African as Christian), *rooleje* 'chopped meat stuffed in sausage skins', *rolliche* 'a sort of sausage', *hoople* 'children's rolling hoop', *boonder* 'to brush away', *pease* 'disgusted', *grilly* 'chilly', *plock* 'to settle down', *blummie* 'a flower', and *speck* 'fat'. Mencken, who provided the above list, also speculated that *hunky-dory* may have come from the Dutch *honk* 'a goal in a game' and took the *Dictionary of American English* to task for failing to list derivatives from *spook: spookiness, spookism, spookologer,* and *spooky*.

Most of the words adopted from Dutch have been so completely domesticated in American English that no feeling of exoticism adheres to them—although, of course, some of them are limited to special groups like older residents of the Hudson Valley. A word like *dope,* from a

Dutch word meaning 'liquid', provides an excellent example. With its derivatives *dope addict, dope fiend, dope
head,* and *dope peddler,* it has assumed an increasing importance in the American vocabulary. The more or less
basic American meaning 'narcotic' had by 1872 been extended to the general sense of 'a preparation for which a
more accurate name is not available'. By 1903, it could
mean any kind of liquid, as in *fly dope.* The compound
dope bucket 'a bucket full of lubricant' (1898) in railroad
jargon got the further meaning 'straight information' or
'consensus of expectations' in sports writing. *Dope* in the
sense of 'information or knowledge, especially of a kind not
widely disseminated or easily available' was current by
1901. *To kick over the dope bucket* 'to perform contrary
to expectations' was in use on sports pages by 1944, while
dope sheet, a collection of information about participants
in a sporting event, especially a horse race, has been used
since 1903. It seems reasonable, therefore, that a horse inspired the "kicking over" metaphor. *Dope sheet* was, however, applicable to other domains, like the stock market,
by 1931. *Dope* meaning 'a person under the influence of
or addicted to the use of some form of dope or drug' (1909)
was extended to mean 'a silly or stupid person'. Comedi-
enne Gracie Allen pretended to have an editorial column,
"Your Daily Dope," punning on two of the derivative
meanings. (The column was part of her comedy pretense
of running for President in the election of 1940; the
humorous "dope" aspect of her character was illustrated
by her decision to "let George [her husband, George Burns]
write my column *Your Daily Dope* because my typewriter
doesn't spell very well when I use it.")

In addition to borrowings *from* the Dutch, American
English has a number of words and compounds referring
to the Dutch. Some of them, however, are probably applicable to Germans ("Deustche") rather than to Hollanders. *Deutsche* is also the term half translated, half

adapted phonetically, in "Dutchman Stories" (wherein, for example, *tam harricoon* means 'damn raccoon') in backwoods folk tales.[20] One's "Dutch" may mean one's temper, and it seems significant that the first citation in *The Dictionary of Americanisms* is:

> It woke Colonel John Forney up to the very highest pitch of his fighting "Injun," or, as they say in Pennsylvania, his "Dutch."

The reference to Pennsylvania suggests that Dutch actually meant German.

In the group of words and phrases referring to the Dutch, there are some that are obsolete or restricted to local usage. Nevertheless, they are important because they helped to differentiate American English from other varieties of the language. *Dutch bake-oven,* most commonly called *Dutch oven* today, was used around 1853: oil-field workers in many parts of the country have adapted the latter phrase to mean 'the forechamber of a gas-fired boiler that provides an incandescent surface for lighting when turned on'. *Dutch barn* (1772) and *Dutch beer saloon* (1887) illustrate the persistence of phrases referring to the Dutch in the description of buildings, as do *Dutch grocery* (1886) and *Dutch doggery* (1835) 'a low or poorly kept hotel, especially for sailors'. *Dutch grass* (1671) and *Dutch cane* (1895) referred to plants that were a nuisance to farmers. *Dutch permain* (1837) was a variety of pear found in New York and New Jersey; *Dutch pike* (1856) was a synonym for catfish; *Dutch pung* (1852) is an obsolete New England term for a sleigh or sledge. In connection with the last, the Dutch themselves probably took *pung* over from the Indians and passed it on to English speakers. A *Dutch sleigh* (1762) had two double seats on steel runners. A *Dutch turnpike* (1818) was made over a swamp by laying trunks of small trees close together.

Most of these phrases were restricted to the Northeastern part of the United States, but there are some surprises. It is surprising how often one runs into *doggery*, for example, in documents concerning the early history of the Pacific Coast.

Significantly, most of these words were adopted into English in the middle of the nineteenth century, when "bad English and worse Dutch" prevailed in the New York–New Jersey area. Very little remains from the colonial period, and nothing from the period immediately after New Amsterdam fell into the hands of the English. The existence of the contact variety of Dutch played an important part in the transmission, just as the existence of Pidgin English played an important part in the transmission of Indian words. The Dutch were one of the more important of the many language groups that made American English what it is, and the study of relationships with Dutch is vitally important to the study of the language.

Of course, there have been later Dutch immigrants to the United States. Since 1900, more than 80,000 have settled in western Michigan, mostly in an area between the Kalamazoo and Grand rivers. Primarily farmers, they occupy deep bottom lands suitable for producing vegetables that can be taken to market, but they do not trap the beaver. One of the towns—named, appropriately enough, Holland—is said to be the "center of Dutch influence in the United States."[21] Although Dutch-language newspapers are printed there, the people in general have adapted themselves to the American way of life, and their linguistic influence on American English has been virtually nonexistent.

There are two possible reasons why their pattern has been so different from that of the early Dutch colonists: first, the colonial Dutchmen had temporal priority, which is always important in a language situation; second, the Creole Dutch language variety was present in the early days. Of the two, the latter was surely the more important. The give-and-take between English and Dutch that was characteristic of the colonial period no longer existed by the time Holland, Michigan, was settled. The new arrivals had to worry about learning English; none of the descendants of Englishmen in the same area had to bother about Dutch. And Indian languages were no longer a factor. The medium of easy transmission between languages, the contact language, had vanished—and so did the influence.

3

Prelude to the West: New Orleans and Louisiana

Treatments of American English usually start on the East Coast, at about the place where the Dutch first settled what became New York, and go overland to the West. Predictably, they discover that linguistic patterns follow the western migration patterns of the British immigrants. If, however, we made the trip by water, we might get some different insights.

A major feature of the port of New York is Brooklyn, and as anyone who knows anything at all about American English is aware, people from Brooklyn have a distinctive way of speaking. They say "toity-toid street" where other people say "thirty-third," and their conversation is sprinkled with "dems," "deses," "doses," and "youse guys" or "yez guys." There are some things wrong with this oversimplified view, as we will see later, but the information is functional enough as practical dialect knowledge, even though the Brooklynite is by no means alone in any of these usages, and there are many Brooklynites who use none of them.

We can leave aside *dem, dese,* and *dose,* since speakers of all kinds of dialects "can't pronounce their *th*'s"—or at any rate don't. Since English has become virtually the world's second language, these particular pronunciations (or something very like them) can be heard as far away as the Philippine Islands or Bujumbura, Burundi. The "oi" of "toity-toid" is a boid of a different color. Its use has been reported from Liberia, Watling Island (the one Columbus first called El Salvador), Frenchtown in Charlotte Amalie, St. Thomas in the U. S. Virgin Islands, the Florida Keys (where it is used by the so-called Conches), the coastal inlet area of North Carolina around Swansboro, and New Orleans. This is a wide range of locations, with only one thing in common: they are all coastal or insular. With the renewed interest in maritime language varieties, it might be instructive to look at a couple of these locations more closely.

If we travel by sea from Brooklyn to New Orleans, we find many things changing, and the dialect is one of the more noticeable. Everyone knows that the languid, drawling Louisianians from the swamps and bayous talk differently from the hustling, pushy New Yorkers whose environment is made up of the potholes and subways of Manhattan. It may be a surprise, then, to get off the boat in New Orleans and find a taxi driver who says "boid" and "toid" in a manner strikingly similar to that of the man who drove you to the docks in New York. It turns out that the New Orleans driver isn't a migrant either; his family has been in New Orleans for several generations.

As a fifty-eight-year-old native of New Orleans explained to me, there are three types of "Louisiana-ese": "Cajunese, spoken with a lot of grunts and groans . . . [sometimes] so heavy that you can't understand it, due to the intrusion of French and Indian phrases"; "North Louisiana-ese [which, according to this informant, has no characteristics prominent enough to be expressed in the local stereotype]"; and "New Or-yuns-ese, which sounds most like Brooklynese." We will return to the first two groups later in this chapter. For the moment let us consider the New Orleanians who impress not only visitors but lifelong residents of the city as speaking something very like "Brooklynese."

Careful listening reveals differences, of course; for one

thing, the New Orleans driver says "you all" or "y'awl," which the Brooklyn taxi driver would be thrown out of the mid-Manhattan taxi driver's haunt at the Belmore Cafeteria for uttering.[1] The New Orleans driver also uses terms like *bayou* and *rigolees* which are virtually unknown to Brooklynites. What are *blocks* in New York City may be *ilets* ('little islands') in New Orleans, the usage tracing back to the time when the inadequate drainage system could not handle the standing water after a heavy rainstorm.

Until very recently, any visiting motorist who asked the New Orleans driver whether standing was permitted in a traffic zone would have been assumed to have lost his control of language. Until a recent national standardization campaign, it was "No Parking" in New Orleans, as in most of the nation, not "No Standing" as in New York, where *No Parking* has a specialized meaning. Standing or not standing was a matter of what was permitted on a *street* or *highway* for the Brooklynite; for the New Orleans driver it might be a *pave*, a *paving*, or a *banquette*. What's alongside the street may be a *pavement* for the Louisiana native, although it's a *sidewalk* for the New Yorker—and for most Americans. Since the supra-regional General American vocabulary has come to New Orleans as well as to other cities, however, these localisms are used less frequently than in earlier years.

Perhaps the most striking similarity between the Brooklyn cabdriver and his New Orleans colleague is the diphthongal vowel nucleus where the English spelling has a vowel followed by *r*: *bird, thirty-third, church, Murphy*. A prominent dialectologist tells us that it or something similar

is used in America in several areas along the Atlantic Coast and the Gulf of Mexico, Eastern New England, metropolitan New York, eastern Virginia, and an extensive belt extending from South Carolina westward as far as eastern Texas and Arkansas. These areas contain about one third of the population of the United States.[2]

The first thing we notice is that the prominent dialectologist has elected to go overland rather than taking our sea route, thereby missing New Orleans and the Florida Keys, not to mention Liberia. The second is that although he assures us that about one-third of the population of the United States lives in areas where this articulation is used, our own impressions suggest that far less than one-third of them use it.

In order to evaluate the contradictory evidence—to decide whether we're going to trust our own ears or the authority of the prominent dialectologist—we will have to formulate the problem somewhat differently. The pronunciation suggested by the spelling *boid* and *toity-toid* is largely a matter of linguistic folklore; we need to have better guidelines if we are to deal rationally with as important a problem as what evidence to trust about sounds.

Folklore tells us a great deal about Brooklyn—about its now-lost Dodgers (more affectionately known as "dem bums") and the importance they once had in the borough's sporting and emotional life. It's a fact that one of the great pitchers for the team was a left-hander named Waite Hoyte; but it's folklore that when he was hit on the left arm by a line drive, the fans rose as one man and screamed, "Oh, my god! Hurt's hoyt!"

Brooklynites don't really pronounce *hurt* as "hoyt"— or Hoyte as "hurt." They don't pronounce *oysters* as *ersters* either—nor *bird* the way most of us say *boid* (thus ruining the other story about the Brooklyn schoolboy who, told by his teacher that a sparrow wasn't a "boid," protested: "But it choips like a boid.")

To be the least bit technical for a moment, what they actually articulate in words like *hurt, bird,* and *third* is a

diphthong that begins in a central position and then glides
up. We can symbolize that pronunciation with /əy/. What
you and I (perfectly *standard* speakers, of course!) do with
our diphthong in *boid* and *oil* can be represented with
/ɔy/. (Actually, I'm a working-class Texan by birth, so
I can have trouble with that second element before *l*—
especially if I'm tired or excited or drunk. When I use it
in my least formal style, people who don't know my dialect
well think I'm pronouncing *oil* and *all* identically.)

Since most of us don't pronounce the Brooklynite's or
the New Orleans cabdriver's /əy/, we tend to hear what
they say as being identical with our own /ɔy/. Except—
and here's the exception that proves hell out of the rule—
when the Brooklynite becomes self-conscious about his
language, which may happen if he gets within a block of
an English teacher or a speech professor or someone who
has written a book on how the English language may not
survive American usage, he tries to "correct" himself.
Since most people are not very good at correcting their
own dialects, he may be overcorrect (we call that process
hypercorrection or *hyperurbanism*). In that case, he may
actually say *erster* instead of oyster—or instead of /əystər/,
as he would naturally pronounce it. This hypercorrect
pronunciation figures in newspaper columns like Earl
Wilson's, where the sign-off "That's Earl, brother!" reflects the partial naturalization to New York City patterns
of a native Ohioan. Some hypercorrecting New Orleans
speakers come closer to "arl" than to "earl."

We must observe something else about the vowel nucleus
in question. The dialectologist quoted above, Hans
Kurath, treats a central simple vowel (as you might pronounce in "uhl") and a central vowel followed by an up-
ward glide (that is, a diphthong) as the same phenomenon.
The Brooklyn, New Orleans, and other coastal speakers
have the diphthongal vowel nucleus (almost like "toid"

and "boid"), whereas other speakers (like some East Texans who came originally from Louisiana) have the simple vowel (almost like "uhl"). By regarding the two as identical, Kurath takes away the reportability of the articulation that the folklore reports as "oi." Collapsing the distinction between it and the simple vowel nucleus, he can report it "spoken in those areas in which one-third of the population of the United States live." If the sound can be assumed to have moved across the United States, in an East-West direction, an overland transmission is implied for it historically. There goes our maritime perception!

The difficulty is that it may not be justifiable to throw together the monophthongic and diphthongic realization of vowel plus *r*.[3] Most speakers perceive the diphthongal pronunciation (like that of certain working-class speakers from Brooklyn and New Orleans) as something special, and language study is supposed to explain what native speakers perceive. If the difference between simple vowel and diphthong is significant—and I believe it is the critical issue here—then the /-y/ glide may be the element that correlates with maritime distribution. Dialectologists acknowledge that there's nothing like it in the regional dialects of England.

If we listen to the New Orleans speaker long enough, we will get a great deal of information that dispels our initial uncanny feeling of having somehow wound up in the port of New York. If we can get him to talk about sandwiches, he may recommend a *poorboy* (without the *r*—"po'boy"), which the Brooklyn driver would call a *hero*. A resident of New Orleans is also more likely to eat *crawfish* than a Brooklynite, who would call it *crayfish*. Both forms came from the French *crêvisse* before the English settled in America, but only the Louisiana resident would ever call the same orthopod a *mud-bug*. The New Orleans native calls his sausage *boudin,* from the

French, a usage now limited to that area, although it was widely reported among Western trappers of the nineteenth century.

New York City is, as everyone knows, one of the most cosmopolitan cities on earth, inhabited by diverse ethnic and linguistic groups, all of whom have influenced the vocabulary. A New York cabdriver may either be Jewish himself or have had enough exposure to Yiddish-tinged English to know words like *lox* and *bagels,* or *goy* and *yenta.* A New Orleans driver might have read enough to have the first two in his passive vocabulary, but he wouldn't normally use them in his conversation. The last two wouldn't be in his vocabulary at all; he would say *gentile* and *gossipper.*

New Orleans, however, also has claims to being a cosmopolitan city. Spanish rule from 1776 to 1800 left its cultural and linguistic traces, most obviously in the names of many of the streets. Irishmen, who began coming around 1790, were responsible for a district still called the Irish Channel, although the ethnic composition of the area is no longer clear-cut. Some 34,000 Germans arrived in 1853–54, although relatively few of them stayed. But French retained the advantage conferred by primacy, and all the other groups were at least partly Gallicized. When we finally isolate what is distinctive about the Louisiana working-class speech, we may find that what differentiates them from their Brooklyn sound-alikes is French. The French have been prominent in New Orleans for about as long as there have been English speakers in New York. There have been three recognizable groups of Louisiana French speakers: the aristocratic speakers of Standard French, the Cajuns (Acadians), and the Black speakers of what some people call "Gombo." To the general populace the first is "Creole" French; to linguists, the last.

The "Gombo" and Cajun speakers provide a lot of evidence for the thesis that maritime language varieties are important in the history of American English, although only the former came to New Orleans by sea. The Cajuns came overland from Nova Scotia in the 1760's, fleeing from the new British overlords of the area, only to come under English-speaking domination again when Napoleon sold Louisiana to the United States nearly forty years later. But when the Cajun wanted to give an account of crossing the prairies, the verb he used was *naviguer* 'to navigate'; he would *embarquer* on buggy trips and 'moor' his horse at the end of them. He even "set sail" *(méttait la voile)* on land. Several sources tell us how a Cajun's daughter all dressed up to be married was described in the terms, *"N'est-ce pas qu'elle une goelétte bien gréée?"* 'Isn't she a well-rigged out little boat?' The Gombo dialect, spoken primarily by Black descendants of West African slaves, probably originated in a maritime trade version of French—with a heavy overlay of West African language influence. And since many sailors still put in at New Orleans, printed invitations to "Sink Your Hook Here" were commonplace in Louisiana saloons well into the 1930's.[4]

Before English came to be dominant in Louisiana, the Blacks and Indians (a mixture so commonplace there that the term *redbone* was coined for 'a person of Indian and Negro parents') used French or "Gombo" as a lingua franca. Some Louisiana Indians still speak French and little or no English. A poor Black New Orleans resident has the grammatical characteristics of Black English; but he or his ancestors quickly learned to say *banquette* for 'sidewalk', *pave* for 'highway', and *flottant* for 'soft prairie with water underneath'. Although Blacks in Brooklyn are almost never taken for "boid" speakers, those in New Orleans frequently use that articulation.

The New Orleans working-class resident who lives in the Irish Channel is likely to differ from his Brooklyn counterpart partly because he lives in proximity to the swamps. He is more likely to fish, and even to hunt alligators. The river boat he goes out in is a *pirogue.* The word is taken, according to William A. Read's *Louisiana French,* from the mainland dialect of the Carib Indian language, being most immediately a Gallicization of Spanish *piragua.* M. LePage Du Pratz's 1758 *History of Louisiana* refers to it in the form *pettaugre.* If he happens to want to command a cow to move to a given place, he will say "La!" French for 'there'. And if he's really bucolic, he will know various calls to animals probably carried over from dialectal French: *choo(ey)* or *choon(ey)* for pigs, *cha* or *'ci (boss)* for cows, *mus* or *tit mus* for calves, *kee, keetie,* or *pee(p)* for chickens.[5]

The Louisiana resident *gets down* (from the French *descendre*) *from* rather than *off* a bus or river boat, and *gets up* rather than *on,* perhaps influenced by the French verb *monter,* although natives of West Indian islands where there is no such obvious source of French influence use the same locution.

Instead of a *wardrobe,* the Louisianian has an *armoire* (pronounced like *armor*). When he reads the paper, it is likely to be the *Times-Picayune,* the second word of which comes from the small French-derived coin that used to be enough money to buy the paper. At a still earlier period, "for a picayune (six cents) a boatman could get a drink, a woman, and a bed for the night"[6]—although he could apparently be robbed of everything he had if he patronized such a cheap joint. It's all a great deal more expensive now.

Except for these vocabulary relics, there are relatively few remnants of French in New Orleans today. If our cab driver talks about the fruit of *Diospyros virginiana,* he probably calls it a "persimmon." In an earlier time he would have called it *plaquemine,* and the tree on which it grew a *plaqueminier.* The base word comes from Illinois *piakimin* through the Mobilian dialect; it is thus obviously cognate with *persimmon,* although considerable language mixing has gone on. There is still a Plaquemine Parish in Louisiana, and a village called Plaquemine Brulee, 'burned persimmon'. But the use of the Indian-French term for the fruit is virtually dead.

French yielded to English slowly and reluctantly in New Orleans and most of the rest of the state, even after Louisiana was sold to the United States in 1803. In the beginning, French speakers proudly insisted upon the use of their language for all official functions, such as in the courts. Since the Anglo-Saxons were also determined that their language should serve these functions, there were often *impasses* over the use of language, with each side pretending not to understand the other. A nineteenth-century article on "The New Orleans Bench and Bar" reported that

> those [Frenchmen] who had succeeded in mastering the "foreign idiom" as the English was then called, affected to use it only when they could not do otherwise, and only on rare occasions.[7]

Such factors complicated courtroom cases, where the French-speaking jurors might go for a stroll and a smoke while an attorney presented his case in English. Angered, the English-speaking jurors would reciprocate:

> Seghers had hardly said a few words in French when the Anglo-Saxon jurors, on their application for a similar favor, were also permitted to stretch their legs under the same arcades.[8]

Under these conditions, something had to give. Linguistic accommodation to French did take place, but English retained its dominance. An occasional attorney had to call on "those French words which he recollected":

"Vous, monsieur, for plaintiff, eh?" McCarty shook his head negatively. "For defendant?" McCarty gave an affirmative nod. "Eh, bien, nous aussi (well, we too)," continued the Saxon . . . as well as he could, whilst he pointed to his two friends as concurring in his opinion.[9]

In this case, and undoubtedly in many others, a bilingual judge prevented complete collapse:

> a short charge was delivered by the judge in English and French, and the jury retired to their room.[10]

In the early years of the nineteenth century, mixing English and French was the conventional solution to the language problem, especially for those of lower station who had neither the aristocratic standing of the old French families nor the wealth of the Anglo-Saxon businessmen. The works of George Washington Cable are rich in such attestations, like this one from "Posson Jones" in *Old Creole Days* (written in 1876, but with the action set in 1815):

> "If I could make juz *one* bet," said the persuasive St. Ange, "I would leave this place fas'-fas', yes. If I had thing—*mais* I did not soupspicion this from you, Posson Jon' . . ."

Or this one from "Madame Delphine," in the same collection, a short story in which both interlocutors speak a heavily Frenchified English:

> He took pains to speak first, saying, in a reassuring tone, and in the language he had last heard her use:
>
> " 'Ow I kin serve you, Madame?"
> "Iv you pliz, to mague dad bill change, Miche."

In New Orleans itself, the dominance of English was established by the mid-twentieth century, so that French is readily apparent to the visitor only in street names and terms on the menu. For "Anglo-Saxons," like the one in the courtroom scene quoted above, French cuisine seemed a much more natural domain for the language than the courtroom:

> I have today a fat turkey *aux truffes* . . . and exquisite claret just received from Bordeaux.[11]

Of course, other groups besides English speakers came to complicate French dominance in Louisiana. A group of Germans arrived in the early days, producing a French-German mixture on the so-called German Coast and giving their name to the *Bayou des Allemands*. Some of the families still have translated German names: La Branch 'branch' from the German name Zweig.[12] During the Spanish regime, a name like Jacob Wilhelm Nolte could be transformed into Don Santiago Villanol.

In the interior, along the bayous, there are still Cajuns, for whom the switch to English is far from complete. We need not turn to fiction for examples of their speech and expressions of their ideals and customs, such as an extreme sense of honor that can lead to a duel. A 1944 book reports one of them as saying:

> "You dance twice in succeed with my girl and I want my satisfied."[13]

Very nonstandard English, with an obvious admixture of French, is regularly attested in the works of favorite nineteenth-century fiction writers of the area, like Kate Chopin:

"I tell you, Pa-Jelf, its neva been no thief in the Bedaut family. My pa say he couldn't hole up his head if he think I been a thief, me."

" . . . any one of the Dortrand girls would have been glad to marry you. But no, nothing would do; you mus' come out on the rigolet for me."

"We got to rememba she ent like you an' me, po' thing, she's one Injun, her."[14]

These attestations can easily be matched from the works of nonfictional reporters:

"Fifty baby chick peep-peein' in a brooder in the hull of my camp! For a whole season I couldn't stand it . . . I buil' a house, me."[15]

Less well known than the Cajuns are certain American Indian groups who have been forced, over the centuries, to make linguistic adaptation to first French and then English. Carolyn Ramsey's novel *Cajuns on the Bayous* (1957) describes the group on the ironically named Isle of Paradise under the rule of their Chief Naquin:

Faces of these islanders were of a startling mixture. Brown of Indian, white of French, tawny Portuguese, mulatto-slave, Asiatic yellow . . . all the nondescript inheritance of long-ago Lafitte men . . . they were there in various combinations, pure in some and faded in others.[16]

One youth, a favorite of the chief, had been away to school and spoke more English than the others. Ramsey observes that he spoke "a French-Indian patois that was different from any I had heard in South Louisiana," and gives us a sample:

About the treasure, *Mam'selle* . . . We looks for her,
yes . . . but da bad spirits no like that. They drive us
away . . .[17]

Even what is known as the French quarter of New
Orleans now has a plurality of inhabitants of Italian de-
scent.[18] The more prestigious groups have, of course,
been most successful in adapting themselves to English.
But even they have kept a French residue. Harnett Kane
tells us how the "Anglo-Saxons have picked up French
locutions unconsciously, saying things like 'I don't gumbo
that French at all.' "[19] And a street called *Desiré* by the
French is so Anglicized that one can read the sentence
Frenchmen Desire Good Children on a street map of the
city, referring to three street names.

The mixture with French has been accompanied by
subtler mixtures from other languages. *Bayou,* the word
we think of as typically Louisianian, comes from Choctaw
by way of French. *Lagniappe,* used fairly generally now
for 'something extra', was originally from Quechua, transmitted through the Gombo-speaking Negroes. Structurally,
the word combines article and noun into one noun base,
which is a marked characteristic of the Creole languages in
general.

We don't really know where *bulldoze* came from, although we are quite sure that the verb preceded *bulldozer,*
the name for the machine, by several decades. Most probably Black speakers are responsible at least for its transmission, since it is widely current in Black speech and in
blues lyrics like "I got a woman; she's pretty but she's
too bulldozing." John Bartlett, whose 1877 *Dictionary of
Americanisms* is the nearest thing we have to an on-the-
spot reference work, traced the word to New Orleans,
where, he asserted, it referred to the actions of a group of
white men who practiced political intimidation upon

Negroes. Although the historical dictionaries now reject Bartlett's history of the word, there are citations from New Orleans around 1877 that support it. There are also attestations of the same word, with the same meaning, in Connecticut and in New York City at about the same time. It seems obvious that this is one of those seaboard words that reflect the early linkage between the port of New York, New Orleans and other points on the Atlantic Coast. The violent actions involved in *bulldozing* explain how *bulldozer* was felt to be appropriate, at a later time, for a machine that pushed everything out of its way and had no time for subtleties.

It is the French-derived word structures, however, that give the area its characteristic flavor. In spite of some problems with phonology, *poorboy* (the sandwich) has no better etymology than *pourboire* 'a tip'. In the oil fields of Louisiana and East Texas, *poorboy* has become a verb meaning 'to get by on a shoestring'. Many other elements of the dialects of Northwestern Louisiana have either spread to those of East Texas or have always been shared by the two. In both, for example, *coal oil* has long been used to mean 'kerosene'.

Although New Orleans was in a sense the first of America's melting pots, the incompleteness of the melting can be seen there even more easily than elsewhere.[20] The Blacks and Indians were banished to a kind of low-caste status, and nobody paid any attention to their language until very recent times; while the Cajuns were left in a geographical isolation in which the language shift to a kind of English went more slowly than it did with other groups. Students with French names in the colleges of Northwestern Louisiana still bring the same structures described above to their English classes.

All but the most assimilated groups, in fact, have kept some French words and structures. By the twentieth century, the sentence-final *moi,* used for emphasis, was restricted to a few groups; but the English word *me* (I don't like that, me) served in the same function. Kane asserts that this structure was so prevalent among the Irish of the New Orleans Irish Channel that "If they didn't add 'me' you knew they didn't mean it."[21] Furthermore, according to Kane, the Irish "even began to shrug and gesture as if they were taking in French along with the air they breathed."[22]

Some Louisianians still say *make a birthday* ("My daughter made fifteen last week"). French names have, especially in the North, undergone strange changes: De-Blieux becomes "Double-you," Breazeale becomes "Brazil," and Fortier "Foshee" (sometimes even in spelling). A guide on the most recent tour of the Natchitoches Historical Society referred to a bidet in one of the old houses as a "buy-day" (rhyming with *eye day*.) Surviving pockets of Spanish speakers have transmitted some of their lore to the surrounding "Anglos," but the familiar Mexican folktale figure La Llorona ('the crying woman') has become Lorna for the English speakers. Under these sociolinguistic conditions, some of the speakers of the area might be skeptical if they were told that some of their language structures had a French origin. A complex set of cultural and sociohistorical factors has determined how many of the French-derived forms any one person may use. Technology and modern custom have made some of them archaic (*lagniappe* is the regrettable example; businessmen using aggressive modern methods don't give anything extra any more).

Nevertheless, it is worth taking a cab ride in New Orleans just to listen to the driver. If he is a working-class resident of the Irish Channel, he may speak something strikingly like "Brooklynese." And it deepens one's perspective on the history of American English to realize that in earlier centuries the explorers and frontiersmen who started from that same point and went up the Mississippi River and out into the Western wilds were subject to the same language-contact patterns.

4

A Nation
of Gamblers

As the meeting place of the second largest salt waterway and the largest fresh waterway easily accessible to nineteenth-century Americans, New Orleans was the single most important town in the movement toward the West. Down the Mississippi came river boatmen in flat boats, crude characters from "Kaintuck" ("half-horse, half-alligator" is only one of the many contemporary descriptions), and wilderness dwellers long out of contact with the softening influence of civilization. There were special vice districts, like Storyville, to contain them; but they were obviously a disruptive influence on the French gentility of the city, and they contributed to the Creoles' unwillingness to accept American ways and the English language.

Although they were not aware of the role they played, the rivermen were part of the big commercial enterprise of developing the frontier and the West. They didn't make a lot of money compared to their shrewder employers, but they had enough to spend at the end of a trip. And, like cowboys at the end of a trail drive or fur trappers at the end of a season, they spent most of it on whoring, drinking, and gambling.

In nineteenth-century New Orleans, the common pastime of the highest and the lowest—even of the slaves— was gambling.[1] The heterogeneous nature of the gamblers provided a wide range of exotic influences on the games played, and it is therefore no accident that it was in New Orleans that a European (probably French, although some would claim it was German) game named *poque* was combined with a Persian game called *As Nas* to form what eventually became the most characteristic game of the American West and perhaps of the United States. *As Nas,* played with five cards in each hand, was obviously introduced by the large numbers of sailors who came into the port of New Orleans; *poque,* limited to three cards per hand, was apparently popular with the New Orleans Creole population from the earliest days. The English game of *Brag,* with early American variations, added the device of making certain cards "wild"—originally such cards were known as "braggers."

The new game caught on first in the dives (after all, not even a river boatman, in spite of the Mike Fink tradition, could spend *all* his time whoring and fighting) and eventually spread up the Mississippi.[2] In *Domestic Manners of the Americans,* Mrs. Trollope reported that "no boat left New Orleans without having as cabin passengers one or two gentlemen whose profession it was to drill the fifty-two elements of a deck of cards to profitable duty."

Although poker eventually reached the big Eastern cities, it was not until well after the date of the Louisiana Purchase (1803). In 1835, a reform administration in New Orleans drove out many of the professional gamblers, and some of them emigrated to cities like New York.[3] But the game had already spread up the Mississippi and into the West. Thus the movement of poker terminology was from West to East, South to North.

As the game spread into the great inland section of America, it took its gradually developing terminology along. New Orleans was the supply base for movements up the Mississippi and to the West, including the U.S. Army's movement into Mexico for the war of 1845. As a consequence of our involvement in that war, poker was not only introduced into the Army but went with the soldiers to other populations as far west as the California gold fields—which we took from Mexico, along with the then less profitable parts of California, in the same war. The words and phrases characteristic of poker were soon current all over the West. We cannot be certain that any one of them originated in New Orleans, but that is the most likely place to look for their origins.

In the West, games like poker and faro (which is of relatively exotic origin itself, since the name may come from *Pharaoh,* a Pharaoh being pictured on one of the cards) assumed an importance they never had elsewhere. They were focal points for the social life of an area and almost a religion. Betting, whether on card games or not, was so much a part of the vocabulary of the "new country" (the West) that, according to travel writer Albert D. Richardson, "you bet" became the standard strong affirmative. A popular nineteenth-century joke was about a man who found a burglar trying to enter his house and pulled out his revolver, shouting "You get!" The answer came instantly: "You bet!" In another story, this one attributed to Mark Twain, a Westerner charged with telling a newly widowed wife about the death of her husband inquires, "Does Joe Toole live here?" and when she nods, replies, "Bet you he don't!"

Poker became such an integral part of the West that its foreign origin and even its association with New Orleans and the Frenchmen of that city were forgotten. The Western players were nevertheless operating in a linguistic environment in which both French and Spanish were prominent. This is reflected in the names of some of the cards: no poker player would ever call an *ace, deuce,* or *trey* a one, two, or three.

The West's own contribution to the game was the invention of stud poker, played with one card down and four cards up. There has been a great deal of speculation about the origin of the name, but the easy explanation—that it comes from *stud* 'a stallion', which was the bet when the game was first played—belongs strictly to etymological folklore. There is a slightly better chance of truth in the story that the expression *a dead man's hand* (a pair of aces and a pair of eights) originated because that was what "Wild Bill" Hickok was holding when he was shot.

Poker was a big thing with the cowboys, marshals, sheriffs, and badmen of the West, and its terminology became a basic part of their vocabulary. There is ample evidence that many expressions that have worked their way into our daily life came from the game. Phrases like *put up or shut up* and *I'll call you on that* (or *I'll call your bluff*), heard frequently and in a great variety of contexts, both derive from poker.

Today, "passing the buck" is more generally associated with politics than with poker, perhaps thanks to Harry Truman's famous slogan: "The buck stops here." The term, however, came into existence on the Western frontier in the 1860's. A player who did not care to deal passed an object on to the next player. This object was frequently, if not always, a knife made with handles of buck horn. The one who passed it on was thus "passing the buck."

Faro was almost as popular in the West, but it was a simple game of luck (based on what happened to be the second card turned up) and lacked the combative appeal of poker, especially the bluffing. It has practically disappeared from the American scene, but it has left what historian Herbert Asbury calls "a very considerable philological contribution to American culture."[4] A person proud of his predicting ability may endeavor to *call the turn* without thinking of card games at all, but the phrase originated in faro and meant 'guess correctly the order of appearance of the last three cards'. (*The Dictionary of*

Americanisms lists the earliest occurrence as 1889, but faro terms in general were current as much as twenty years before that date.) Anyone who *plays both ends against the middle* owes the descriptive terminology for the action to a dealer's method of providing for a kind of double bet by a faro player. There was also a system of playing a card to win and lose an even number of times, which was called *breaking even*. The term was probably current in the West by 1860. Today every American business that undertakes a new venture calculates a *break-even point,* a term that does not appear in any historical dictionary.

One way of beginning a business or a game is *on a shoestring* 'with a small amount of money or capital'. *The Dictionary of Americanisms* has this term no earlier than 1904, but it too comes from faro and so must have been in use at least forty years earlier. If the player who starts with very little is lucky, in faro or in business, he can wind up *on velvet. Velvet* was the faro term for money won from the house. By 1901, Westerners were using the term for 'profit or gain beyond what is usual or expected'. Whether he is making a great deal of money or not, a persistent player or businessman tends to *string along* 'go along with' the game or the business. This term is attested as early as 1790, but it was certainly reinforced by the Westerner's second favorite gambling game, where it meant 'continue playing'.

Today the phrase *in hock* means 'to have one's possessions in a pawn shop'; and since a pawn shop is now called a *hock shop,* there seems to be no reason to look further for the term. But historians of the West tell us that the last card in the faro box was originally known as the *hocketty card* and later was said to be *in hock.* The player who bet the card that turned out to be the last one was at a disadvantage, and therefore by a natural transference was "in hock" himself. Since faro was a gambling game, losing cost money, so *in hock* rapidly came to mean 'at a financial loss'. Among professional gamblers, the phrase developed the special meaning 'beaten by a smarter man'; among thieves, it came to mean 'in prison'.[5] But for the average player it simply meant a situation in which a debt had to be paid and he might have to pawn—or hock—some of his possessions. The place where one might get a loan (at exorbitant interest) on the collateral of a watch or a wedding ring became, naturally enough, the *hock shop*.

In faro, the first card played is called *soda*. This led to a widespread Western phrase *from soda to hock*. Western lexicographer Ramon Adams compares it to the Easternism *from soup to nuts*. It isn't immediately obvious why this phrase failed to catch on the way *in hock* did, but a weak guess would be that the nature of gambling gives a greater intensity of meaning to being broke than to the formalities associated with the beginning and end of a game.

The phrases associated with gambling transfer easily from one game to another. A person can get in hock as easily in a poker game as he can playing faro. And *jackpot*, originally the reward of the rare big winner in poker, is now more familiar as the equally unlikely upshot of playing the slot machine. With its connotations of winning a great deal of money, the term was a natural for radio and television quiz shows and other publicized contests. By extension, *hitting the jackpot* (which of course comes from slot machines, not cards) can mean 'any stroke of luck', not necessarily involving money.

Deal, a word that had been around for a very long time in English, took on a special meaning among the poker players of the West. The basic meaning was 'share' or 'divide' (the word being cognate with the German noun *Teil* and the verb *teilen*). Since the five cards each player receives in draw poker are his share, it was natural to call such a distribution a *deal*. The person who officiated over the sharing of the cards was naturally the *dealer*. From this, *deal* as a verb acquired the meaning 'to apportion the cards'—a back formation from *dealer*. The noun *deal* was then used for the apportioning of the cards, a specialization of its earlier meaning. And from that came terms like *square deal* and *new deal*. But in American usage *deal* also came to mean any transaction or arrangement, a regeneralization that was helped along by the faro meaning, 'twenty-five turns'.

Square deal, long familiar in the West and on the Mississippi, was an important slogan in the 1904 presidential campaign of Theodore Roosevelt. It would be a suicidal slogan today, since the 1960's made the word *square* a synonym for naïve or "out of it"; but it meant 'honest' to the Westerner and to Teddy Roosevelt. TR's distant relative Franklin D. Roosevelt was surely aware of the American fondness for poker when he chose the slogan *New Deal.* (For more on this, see Chapter 7.)

Harry Truman, a poker player and a great practical folklorist, chose to call his own program the *Fair Deal.* The cynical expressions "Big deal!" "What a deal!" and "Big dealer!" seem to have been widely current during and just before the Truman administration.

Other poker terms that have passed into the general language include *dealing from the bottom of the deck* 'taking unfair or illegal advantage', *deal me out* 'I don't care to participate in this one', and its reverse, *deal me in*. The cowboy who sat around hoping for a game but not actually participating was, according to Ramon Adams again, *sweatin' a game*—as one might sweat the grades of last semester's work or the results of a blood test. Poker rules often require a hand of minimal quality (for example, a pair of jacks) to open the bidding; thus the phrase *for openers* by extension means a beginning action in any kind of activity.

In poker and in other gambling games, a *piker* is one who is inclined to make small bets. One tradition traces the term to westward migrants from Pike County, Missouri, who came as small farmers and were much less willing to risk their all on a card game than the trappers and cowboys.[6] Whether this is accurate or not, a piker may want to ante very little. (*Ante,* meaning 'before', was of course borrowed from Latin long ago; but the poker sense is an Americanism, from 1835.) He would operate, then, at a *penny ante* level and not put much in the *kitty.* Originally the term for the poker "pot" (whence the expression *to sweeten the pot* 'to increase the stakes'), the term *kitty* came to mean any kind of collected fund. Of unknown origin, the word may well be an Americanism although it is not listed in the dictionaries as such. *The Oxford English Dictionary* records it first from 1892—very late for a poker term. *Feed the kitty* is now an injunction to contribute to any fund and could conceivably be used for a collection in church.

Poker terminology is also reflected in the expression *to go someone one better* 'to raise the bettor, or to excel his performance'. In the 1840's, when the term originated, it might be *five better, ten better,* or any other such number. British usage had known *to go a crown* (or any other sum of money) 'to bet a crown', etc., but the addition of the indirect object and *better* seems to be American.

We are, of course, scornful of the person who never goes anyone one better—a fair definition of a piker, in or out of poker. Our scorn is even greater, however, for the *stool pigeon,* a term adopted in gambling which probably did not originate there. Ramon Adams thought that it came from American gamblers in the late nineteenth century who used it to designate 'a hustler for a faro bank'; but the use of *pigeon* in the sense of 'a bird [real or artificial, literal or figurative] used as a decoy' is attested as early as 1811. By the 1830's, a stool pigeon began to be what it is today—'a police spy'. In this case, faro seems to have specialized a term from American slang rather than creating it.

In poker, the ability to bluff is almost as important as skill in playing or luck in drawing the right cards. The term *bluff* itself may have come from card-playing in the first place. The first use on record seems to be

> Those who play at pharo bark
> At poko [sic], brag, or loo or bluff
> Must all be sure to lose enough.[7]

By 1845, the game could be identified as " 'bluff' or 'poker' ".[8] The person who bluffs too much or whose bluff is exposed, however, occupies the lowest possible position in the estimation of the others. He may even be a *four-flusher*, one who tries to make four cards of the requisite type do the work of five, or to vaunt his other abilities beyond what he can actually accomplish.

The effective reaction to a person suspected of bluffing is to *call his bluff* or *call his hand*. The first recorded use of the latter expression is from San Francisco in 1857:

> Finally, after floating him through a list of metaphors, his good nature gets the best of him; and he concludes to 'call our hand' . . .

By 1876, Bret Harte could write, "But suppose he sees that little bluff and calls ye"—perhaps the very apogee of such expressions.

Because of the importance of bluffing in poker, it is important not to let your opponent guess anything about your hand from your facial expressions. A *poker face* is thus a face that conceals all emotions, and it is useful in many activities other than poker, some of which do not involve bluffing at all. One of the things his opponents found so terrifying about Joe Louis was his complete lack of expression as he approached the other fighter; sportswriters commented endlessly on his poker face, even though everyone knows by now that he wasn't bluffing. Neither was Helen Wills Moody, "Little Poker Face," who dominated women's tennis in the 1920's.

Bret Harte, who called one of his most popular stories "The Outcasts of Poker Flat," provides a great deal of evidence about the importance of poker on the frontier and in the mining camps. In his somewhat deplorable poem, "The Heathen Chinee," the deceptively clever Chinese player gives the lie to the popular phrase *not a Chinaman's chance,* which developed in the Gold Rush of 1849 and spread throughout the West, referring to the fact that Chinese miners were allowed to dig only in worked-out claims where they weren't likely to find any gold.[9]

It must be borne in mind that the communication situation on the frontier was at all times multilingual, and that the English used there, in whatever activity, was not always that of native speakers. This may have been partly why card-playing and betting terminology, which grew out of common activities, became so widespread in their applications. In any case, the terms are now usable in international and highly cosmopolitan contexts. The ideal of stud poker, *aces back to back* (the "hole" card, turned down, is an ace and the first card turned up is an ace), provides a term that has been extended to many fields. The New York *Post* music column for May 23, 1975, for example, described how a noted conductor had presented "back-to-back performances of *Tannheuser* and Schoenberg's *Gurrelieder.*"

If the aces are back to back, then one of them is an *ace in the hole*—generally applicable to any kind of secret but legitimate advantage. Walter McCulloch considered the expression common enough in the logging camps, where a lot of card-playing goes on, to include it in his *Woods Words* with the definition 'a hidden value of some kind'. Originally, *an ace up one's sleeve* (or merely *something up one's sleeve*) indicated that the person was cheating; later, however, the phrase came to mean merely having something in reserve.

A *full house,* three cards of one kind and two of another, is a very good poker hand, since it beats everything except a straight flush and four of a kind. By extension, it can carry a favorable connotation for activities as diverse as having a sold-out performance to producing a large family. A poker player who holds such hands consistently is likely to wind up *in the chips,* 'in the money'. (Asbury, the authority on gambling terminology, reminds us that they were originally called *checks* in poker and that *chips* is a borrowing from faro.) Poker chips are white, red, and blue, in ascending order of value. *Blue chip* now refers to the domain of the stock market, where *blue-chip stocks* (having virtually displaced gilt-edged securities) are the best (as, for example, those measured in the Dow-Jones average). *To cash in one's chips* originally meant 'to leave the game', but poker assumed so much importance for some players that it became a synonym for 'to die'. *Lay 'em down,* literally to lay the cards on the table, also had the connotation 'to die'.

A not-so-sly player may *draw to an inside straight,* 'take a chance that has little possibility of success'. If a dealer *stacks the cards* (arranges them so that he will receive better cards than his opponent), the sucker involved finds *the cards stacked against him* (as he might in a lawsuit in which the judge was the plaintiff's brother). From the point of view of the cheater, however, the deck is well stacked, a term that by extension may apply to many things, including women. A *shuffle* is supposed to scramble the cards so that the dealer does not know which one he is dealing, but the victim of any kind of cheating may be given a *fast shuffle*. Of course, the oldest form of trickery is *dealing from the bottom of the deck,* giving the bottom card to a player rather than the top one. If your professor gave you a test this week from the lesson for next week, he could be accused of the same kind of dealing.

Once the cards have been shuffled and dealt, draw poker allows for the exchange of low-valued cards for some of dimensions still unknown to the drawer or to the honest dealer. A really confident player, however, may chose to *stand pat*—that is, leaving his hand "in the way it fell." (*Pat* in this sense is not an Americanism, but the poker expression is.) A great deal of respect, even awe, goes to the possessor of the *pat hand*. The term *stand pat* is, of course, used in a very favorable sense in many activities, notable among which is politics. "Stand Pat with McKinley" was one of the most successful presidential campaign slogans of American history.

Simple draw poker has a basis of bluff, call, and showdown (when a player is required to reveal his cards and the game is settled). The last term can be appropriately applied to, among other things, the last game in a playoff series in sports, or a confrontation between two major powers in international affairs. The most famous variation of the basic game, aside from stud poker, is to set up some comparatively low-valued card, like the deuce, as a *wild card*. This term, too, has taken on wide applications: the National Basketball Association's play-off involves a "wild card" team, which is lower in won-lost percentages than the other teams in the play-off, and the position enjoyed by such a team is known as the *wild-card berth*.

With the precedent set in the West by faro and poker, American English easily absorbed expressions from other card games. Bridge has been one of the most productive. It is, however, a more cosmopolitan game than poker, and its terms are not so likely to be Americanisms in the narrow sense. The game reached England and America at about the same time, circa 1892, after having been popular in foreign areas like Russia, Turkey, and Egypt. A relatively simple Anglo-Saxon game, whist, was its predecessor in the English-speaking world, but bridge is far more sophisticated and has influenced our terminology much more.

A *long suit* today does not necessarily have anything to do with bridge; it may refer to a decathlon athlete's ability to broad-jump better than he runs the hundred-yard dash, or a linguist's to analyze American Indian languages better than he reconstructs Proto-Bantu. The noun *bid,* in the bridge sense of *a bid of seven spades,* has spread to any attempt to gain an advantage, as in *a bid for fame.* Spades are the highest suit in bridge, so *in spades* has become a general term for the high quality of whatever is under discussion. One *makes points* at the bridge table, but also with a woman or a professor, depending upon the direction of one's interests.

One of the best ways to succeed is to proceed with *finesse*—that is, to take a trick with a lower-valued card while holding the higher-valued one in reserve. The term is used, in the sense of generally intelligent procedures, in domains as distant as boxing: "He taught me what finesse was," bantamweight boxer Bobby Chacon explained in an interview quoted in a UPI press release of June 15, 1975. The opposite of finesse is *trumping one's partner's ace,* taking a trick that already yours.

Every bridge player must *follow suit,* play a card of the same suit that has been led, if he can, and thus *to follow suit* becomes to do what someone else has done: *John ordered a martini and Bill followed suit.* Not to follow suit—not to play a diamond when you have at least one diamond—is to *renege,* now a general term for failure to discharge one's obligations.

It is altogether possible that the verb *to duck,* in the sense of 'back out or default', also developed from bridge.

The usage is first attested in *The Oxford English Diction-ary* from 1896, whereas the bridge term is not represented before 1905. There is no absolute accuracy, however, as the examples of terms from faro and poker given above illustrate, in the dates of the citations as the first use. The bridge term involves forestalling an opponent's long-range plan by playing a smaller card than the one the opposition has led even though holding a higher card. The ducker thus retains long-term control of his suit by refusing a short-term advantage. It is likely that the term *duck* in boxing comes from the same source: the boxer places him-self at the temporary disadvantage of assuming a lower stance in order to avoid the even greater disadvantage of taking a solid punch.

The simpler gambling game blackjack (or "twenty-one," "twenty-one or bust") was also popular in the early West and remains so, as any visitor to Las Vegas can attest. *Hit me,* an injunction to the dealer to add a card to one's total, has some figurative currency as a "sport's" way of staying in the game. *I'm busted,* appropriate when the player has more than twenty-one points, can also indicate that one is out of money or *hors de combat,* but the term could also come from bridge (in which a *bust* is a hand with nothing). In more recent slang, *busted* meaning 'ar-rested' has virtually displaced the older usage.

Slot machines, the prevalent vice of the New West, have given us *hit the jackpot* 'enjoy an extreme, unexpected stroke of luck', adapted from the poker term, and *a lemon* 'an absolute loser' from the appearance of the one symbol that cannot enter into any winning combination.

Dice-playing was not equally important in the West. In *Sucker's Progress,* Herbert Asbury tells us that it "ap-parently never became very popular on the rivers except among the Negro deck hands";[10] and it was not the favorite of the cowboy by any means. Yet cowboy historian Philip Ashton Rollins assures us that the dicer's *at the first rattle out of the box,* as a way of expressing prompt action, was important to cowpunchers.[11] Of the terminology of shooting dice, *eighter from Decatur,* the call when the point is eight, has an extended version:

> Eighter from Decatur
> County seat of Wise.

Wise County is in West Texas (at least, it's west of Fort Worth, which claims to be "where the West begins"), and the charm works only if one chants in the proper rhythmical manner. *Eighter* becomes *Ada* in certain *r*-less dialects, and a folk etymology about a young lady who brings luck to crapshooters has developed.

The call for a point of four is, of course, "Little Joe from Kokomo." Kokomo, Indiana, is close to the Mississippi, and its widespread use in the gambling chant may be due to the influence of river boatmen. Dice players seldom stayed put.

Dice-playing expressions rival those of poker and faro in the extent of their figurative usage. *Snake eyes,* two ones, is the symbol for any kind of impossible predicament. *To crap out* or *craps* is used for any failure or bad luck. *Seven-come-eleven,* on the other hand, is the war cry of the perennially hopeful shooter; a national chain of quick-food stores incorporated it into their name as an obvious way of trading on its favorable associations. Even if the crap shooter doesn't shoot seven or eleven, he can still *make his point*—as can a nongambler at a scholarly convention, with a paper in a professional journal, or in a back-fence argument. In the academic context, a scholar more desirous of making his own theory prevail than of increasing pure knowledge can *load the dice* as easily as he can *stack the cards,* even to the point of setting up an experiment with a self-fulfilling hypothesis.

These Western innovations from gambling terminology

comprise an important contribution to the total American lexicon. If their number is not overwhelmingly large, there is a compensating factor in their productivity and applicability in a large number of figurative contexts.

Of course, not everybody regards these American expressions in a favorable light. So prominent a figure as Edward L. Katzenbach, Jr., former Deputy Assistant Secretary of Defense for Education and Manpower Resources, has asserted that they are "crass" and "inflexible" phrases which lead to "circuitous thinking."[12] Katzenbach believes that we would think straighter and arrange our affairs more efficiently if we were a nation of chess rather than poker players. Edwin Newman, in *Strictly Speaking*, seems to agree in regarding some of the same expressions as regrettable.

The hypothesis that we would be better off if we got the terminology of our informal speech from chess rather than poker is, however, as untestable as the other famous one about how we would have been better off if Grant had surrendered to Lee. If we're Americans talking to other Americans, we have to use the gambling terminology or throw in our hands.

5

Drinking, Smoking, and Chewing Tobacco

L ike other Americans, the frontiersmen—cowboys, trappers, river boatmen—took their vices where they could get them. In the case of fornication, this obviously meant cohabitation with Indian women, except when the "painted women" of New Orleans or Dodge City could be visited. Some of the other vices they carried along with them, since the materials were not readily available on the frontier. Chief among these were liquor and tobacco, which were standard American indulgences back East. Observers like Mrs. Trollope, who sailed for America in 1827 and returned to England in 1831, commented with more than a little disgust:

> During my abode in the country I not only never met a literary man who was a tobacco chewer or a whiskey drinker, but I never met any [men] who were not [literary men], that had escaped these degrading habits.[1]

Since in the West there were only a few like novelist Owen Wister who were "literary men," it would appear that most of the frontiersmen were addicted to those "degrading habits."

The consumption of alcohol was obviously not an American innovation, but every part of the activity in the United States bore the stamp of specifically American practice, and the terminology differed at every point from that of England. Coastal New England, being in a close trade relationship with Barbados and the other West Indian islands, drank a lot of rum. The word is a shortened form of *rumbullion* (of unknown origin), the word used in Surinam, the West Indian islands, and the maritime trade. The drink was also called *kill-devil,* a term so widespread that the French borrowed it as *guildive.* Some of the New England settlers called the drink *ocuby* or *ahcoobee,* in imitation of the Indians' name for it; others engaged in more conventional English compounding and called it *Barbados liquor* or *Barbados brandy.* The word *rum* spread from English into most of the common European languages, probably because of its extensive use at sea as a sailor's liquor ration.

The American frontier and the West, on the other hand, drank whiskey, made not from malted barley (with or without unmalted barley or other cereals) as in the British Isles, but from corn ("maize" or "Indian corn") or rye. Bourbon, made from the American-style corn and named for the county in Kentucky where it was originally distilled, was ever increasingly the dominant type of whiskey; *corn spirits* (1764) was its original name, *corn whiskey* is first attested in 1843, and *corn juice* was used for a time around 1846. Rye whiskey was rare enough that the term, occurring in a folk song, was easily turned into *red whiskey:*

> It's red whiskey, red whiskey, red whiskey I cry
> If I don't get red whiskey I surely will die.[2]

"Red whiskey" was not all that hard to get. Mrs. Trollope wrote:

> Whiskey, however, flows everywhere at the same fatally cheap rate of twenty cents (about one shilling) the gallon,

and its hideous effects are visible on the countenance of every man you meet.[3]

Half-humorous defenders of whiskey would deny its "hideous effects" and proclaim a medicinal value for it. The legendary Davy Crockett saw it in the more characteristically frontier manner:

> Congress allows lemonade to the members and has it charged under the head of stationery—I move also that *whiskey* be allowed under the item of fuel.[4]

Others claimed "medicinal value" as a *snakebite remedy*, a term that has passed into proverbial usage. An early New Orleans "doctor" named Duffy sold *Duffy's Pure Malt Whiskey*, which was guaranteed to make it impossible for any disease to remain in the body.

Terms for whiskey-based drinks were partly indigenous, partly foreign, as in *julep*, a word with Arab and Persian origins. *Julep* had been in British English since 1400, but it meant 'a sweet drink prepared in different (usually non-alcoholic) ways'. It is specifically American in the sense of an alcoholic mixed drink, first attested from Virginia in 1787. The term spread quickly in the United States. *Julep drinkers*, applied to habitués of bars in San Francisco, is attested for the Gold Rush period (1859). *Mint julep*, the most widely used compound, was in existence by 1809; and *mint sling*, the name for another drink involving a sprig of mint, was current by 1804 but seemingly out of fashion after 1840.

Many drinking terms were the products of what Mencken called "the Gothic age of American drinking as of American word making," between the Revolution and the Civil War. A great many fantastic drinks were invented during that period, and some of them were given equally fantastic names. Captain Frederick Marryat observed in 1839 that there were "many other compounds [for mixed drinks] which only the luxuriance of American English could invent." On the other hand, it was the twentieth century that saw the development of *fizz* (with compounds like *gin fizz*), *rickey (gin rickey, rum rickey, rye rickey), sour (whiskey sour, tequila sour), daisy, fix, smash, martini, sidecar, daiquiri, Alexander, screwdriver,* and *white mule* 'gin' (1928). *Manhattan* as a name for a drink is first attested in 1894, and *highball* in the 1890's. The word-forming tendencies that generated these forms had, however, developed earlier. *Cobbler,* according to *The Oxford English Dictionary* 'a drink made of wine, sugar, brandy, and pounded ice, and imbibed through a straw or other tube', is first attested in 1809 (as *sherry cobbler*) in the works of Washington Irving. It next appeared in 1843 in Dickens' *Martin Chuzzlewit.* Martin, whose servant Mark offered to bring him a "cobbler," assumed that a shoe repairman must be involved. *Stone-fence,* made of ginger beer and brandy, is attested from Irving in 1809 and from another American source in 1859. *Whiskey straight* "U.S. slang" according to *The Oxford English Dictionary,* is first known from 1892, in the writings of Mark Twain. Since that time, presumably, *taking it straight* has come to mean not only drinking whiskey (or vodka, gin, etc.) without a mixer but also, metaphorically, taking anything in life as it comes. It is hard to imagine *neat,* the nearest British equivalent, in anything like the same sense.

The word *cocktail* as well as the drink itself originated in America. It is first known from the same citation from Washington Irving that includes *stone-fence* and *sherry cobbler.* By 1834, Tyrone Power (grandfather of the movie actor) could, on a visit from Ireland, appreciate the mixing abilities of a Black man named Cato:

> For Cato is a great man, foremost among cullers of mint,
> whether for *julep* or *hail-storm*; second to no man as a
> compounder of *cock-tail*, and such a hand at a *gin-sling*.

Unfortunately, neither the actor nor the dictionaries tell
us much about *hail-storm*, but Power does give us an interesting fact about the bartender:

> Cato is a gentleman of colour who presides at a little
> tavern some four miles from New York.[5]

It may be no accident that a Black bartender of at least
transitory fame is associated with the early history of the
cocktail. In Krio of Sierra Leone, *kaktel* means 'scorpion'—
a creature with a sting in its tail, which might link
metaphorically with a drink of some impact (compare the
name of a more recently invented cocktail, the *stinger*).[6]
The term was, however, not a new Americanism at the
time Power heard it; in addition to the use by Irving in
1809, there is a recorded attestation from the Hudson,
New York, *Balance* for May 13, 1806. New Orleans tradition, running contrary to the somewhat limited documentation of the dictionaries, celebrates the Crescent City
as the place where the cocktail was invented.[7] Innumerable
compounds like *champagne cocktail, cocktail party,* and
the de-alcoholized *fruit cocktail* came from this addition
to American English and spread rapidly to world-wide
varieties.

The early associations of *cocktail* are obviously Eastern
United States. But all of the early terms came into existence at a time when the frontier was not that far from
the Eastern section of the country, and belong essentially
with the frontier. If the association of *cocktail* with Krio
and therefore with the Pidgin-Creole tradition is significant, it is part of a complex of associations between these

contact varieties and the frontier. Pidginisms like *palaver* and *savvy*, common to Krio and the other Pidgin-Creole varieties, were in general currency in the American West. Canadian Creolist Ian F. Hancock has pointed out how *galoot* and *(kit and) caboodle*, among other familiar Westernisms, parallel *galut* and *kabudu* of Krio.[8] It was in the West, too, that "Here's how" developed as a toast, out of the well-attested Indian greeting, which was also transmitted through Pidgin English. British traveler Richard Burton, in the mid-nineteenth century, made one of the many reports:

> "How! How!" the normal salutation [of the Indians]. It is supposed to mean "good" and the Western man, when he drinks to your health, says "Here's how."[9]

Although the Indian "How!" is widely regarded as the invention of Hollywood or some dime novelist, there is serious evidence that it is genuine. Frontier observer J. H. Cook reported how Indian approbation was expressed: "Yells of 'How!' came from all sides."[10] Later Samuel Bowles, in *Our New West*, reported "*How* is adopted from the Indians as an abbreviation for 'How do you do?' or 'How are you?' " It is, however, erroneous to assume that the form originated in any such abbreviation.

Most often it is taken as representing the English adverb meaning 'in what manner'. This is the way in which toasters interpret it, which has resulted in several stereotyped expansions of "Here's how," like the following from Texas:

> Here's how!
> Did I say how?
> Well, I meant when.
> 'Cause I've known how,
> Since God knows when.

The word *how,* like the weakly suggestive *it* which the movies picked up in the Clara Bow period, sometimes receives a "sexy" intonation—suggesting that sexual ability and knowledge as well as drinking performance may be involved. All this is a recent development; on the frontier, *how* meant most nearly 'good', and *here's how* was an approximate equivalent of 'to your health'.

Where alcoholic consumption was concerned, *how* in the West generally referred to *how much* rather than to *how well.* The cowboy, the trapper, and the sailor were more likely to get lickered up than to sip fine liquor. So, as a matter of fact, was the mistreated associate of the first two, the Indian. *Joy-water* was one of the names befitting such an attitude toward whiskey. *Firewater,* a well authenticated Indianism, was another. This term probably came originally from Algonquian and was transmitted through Pidgin English. The only alternative suggestion would be an unlikely etymological examination of something like *brandy,* the shortened form of *brandywine* from Dutch *brandewijn* 'burnt or distilled wine'. Spontaneous reaction is, of course, not completely out of the question; any drinker who remembers taking his first swig of straight whiskey may be willing to believe that the Indian phrase was purely descriptive. Sow as the frontierism *gut warmer.*

Lacking a cultural tradition for controlling the fermented products of their own and European-imported grains, the Indians frequently manifested the piteous effects of overindulgence. The 1775 *History of the American Indians* by James Adair contains several reports of this general type:

> They [in this case, the Indians of the South, east of the Mississippi] are slow, but very persevering in their undertaking—commonly temperate in eating, but excessively immoderate in drinking.—They often transform

themselves by liquor into the likeness of mad foaming
bears.[11]

Traders in all parts of the country made capital of the
Indians' easy addiction to whiskey, and *Indian whiskey*
was an important trade item. For it, the standards of
quality were even lower than they were for frontiersmen
in general. It has been described as consisting of anything
with a bad taste that induced vomiting, since many Indians
expected to be sick as a result of a drinking bout.

Because the liquor trade with the Indians caused much
disturbance on the frontier, laws against it were passed.
The illegal practice of *bootlegging* developed as a way of
continuing the extremely profitable trade. In the beginning, the whiskey was sold to the Indians in a flat bottle
that could be carried, quite literally, in the leg of a boot.
The term *bootleg,* referring to a portion of the boot, had
existed in American English since 1855, but by 1889–90
both *bootleg* and *bootlegger* referred exclusively to the
practice of carrying liquor in such a way as to avoid police
detection. Later the verb came to mean 'to pirate' or 'to
sell illegally', no matter what the commodity involved. A
1928 citation from Boston tells how "books are boot-
legged." In football, a *bootleg* play is one involving a
certain kind of deception, especially when the quarterback
bootlegs the ball by faking a hand-off to a running back,
keeping the ball hidden from the defense, and running
with it himself. In this case, the feature of deception has
survived whereas the feature of illegality has perished—
the play is in no sense against the rules of football.

The frontiersmen used crude and boisterous terms for
alcoholic drinks. One of the most characteristic is *rotgut*
(1819), a term for something other than the world's
smoothest whiskey. It was obviously in very ordinary usage,
since the shortened form *rot* is also attested. Horace Greeley
observed that

A grocery devoid of some kind of 'rot', as the fiery beverage was currently designated, was to them a novel and most distasteful experience.[12]

Rotgut, redeye, red whiskey, or *tangle-foot whiskey* were what were likely to be in the Westerner's cupboard. Tales were current in the West about the putting down of a stranger with a more educated thirst, who demanded something fancier than *snake poison* or *chain-lightning.* Among other now-obsolete terms for cheap whiskey is *valley tan,* in use primarily in Utah. The connotation was that of homemade whiskey, much the same as *corn whiskey* or *white lightning.* In use between 1860 and the beginning of the twentieth century (with one citation as late as 1942), *valley tan* reflected a use first attested in 1858 in the more general sense of 'every article made or manufactured in the territory'. As the word *tan* suggests, it first referred to leather made there.

Hoe Joe Whiskey, apparently a nonce form, was recorded in 1867, significantly enough in Virginia, Nevada, the heart of the silver-mining country, where rough and tough miners wanted kick and not refinement in their liquor.

Some Americans were so opposed to the consumption of alcohol that they became *saloon smashers* (1901), who went around physically wrecking establishments that sold liquor. *Saloon* itself, in the sense of 'a drinking bar', is originally American, first attested in 1848. In the more general sense of 'a room', the word has been in English since 1728, taken over from the French *salon*—although several other Romance languages have similar forms. The compound *saloon keeper* (dutifully translated 'publican' by British observer G. Campbell, who first recorded it) was around at least as early as 1789. A synonym, *saloonist,* was in vogue around 1882–88. *Barroom* is first attested for America in 1809 in the writings of an English traveler named Kendall, who took the trouble to provide the British equivalent, *tap-room*.

Philip Ashton Rollins confirms the general impression that whiskey was drunk straight on the frontier, and was generally bourbon. The cowboy might experiment with the Mexicans' mescal, but not with any fancy mixed drinks. Rollins tells of the Easterner who said to the frontier bartender, "I guess I'll take a cocktail," and was told, "You don't guess, you drink, and you gets it straight and in a tin cup."[13] Farther east, they drank *moonshine*. This term is not originally American, having been in use in the smuggling trade between England and the continent of Europe from earlier times, but *moonshiner*, the term for the man who makes such whiskey, is.

Westerners described the process of drinking with considerable ingenuity. Owen Wister's *Journal* includes an attestation, in 1894, of "I never drink 'cept when alone or with somebody"—which is still in use, with variations—and "If a man drinks that, he's liable to go home and steal his own pants," now obsolete. The cowboy could afford to be prodigal with such phrases since he created them so easily. If, for example, a brawl developed in the saloon, one cowboy might hit another with his six-shooter and "put a head on him so he could eat hay like a horse."[14]

In spite of all these outward shows of violence, the Westerner was merely *kicking up his heels*. This phrase must surely be of Western origin, although the dictionaries don't show it. The juxtaposition of the words *kick* and *one's heels* has a long history; according to *The Oxford English Dictionary*, a phrase of that composition has been around since 1760, in the sense of 'to wait idly or impatiently'. When the cowboy who had just finished driving a herd over the long trail got his pay, he wanted quick action, not waiting around. For him, the term took on a new significance, perhaps from the way a young colt behaved when *feeling its oats*.

When such "kicking up" involved drinking, as it usually did, it was synonymous with terms like *cut one's wolf loose, dehorn, freight one's crop, hear the owl hoot, lay the dust, keep the double doors swinging.* In one of the characteristic Western borrowings from nautical language (cf. *prairie schooner* and its predecessor *prairie ship, caboose, cache, calaboose*), to take a drink might be to *hoist* ("h'ist") *one.* If the drinker got too much, it was said that *someone stole his rudder.* Hancock has shown the relationship of some of these nautical terms to the vocabulary of Krio of Sierra Leone.[15]

The process of consuming alcohol was simple and direct for the Westerner. He *bellied up* to the bar and *bent an elbow.* Among the loggers, too, according to Walter McCulloch's *Woods Words,* an *elbow bender* was 'a drinking man'. Ramon Adams' *Western Words* gives *wearing calluses on his elbows* for 'spending time in a saloon'. A person who had too much to drink was *booze blind, gypped,* or *alkalied,* although the last could also mean having taken in too much of the mineral material of the wasteland.

The legends of the West stressed the joy-bringing effects of alcoholic beverages rather than the "ruinous" ones preached against by Mrs. Trollope, the saloon smashers, and other tiresomely puritanical meddlers. Liquor "put hair on your chest" by a reverse logic of anatomy no less treasured because of its absurdity. For predominantly young, aggressively masculine groups like the cowboys, long life was no great desideratum anyway; enjoyment of one's transient virility was more important than a tranquil old age. There was a general expectation of *dying with one's boots on*—an expectation so frequently fulfilled that Western cemeteries toward the end of the nineteenth century were known as *boot yards.* (The movies' and novels' *boot hill,* especially in *Gunsmoke,* seems to be a later version.) And if he didn't die young, the heavy carouser of the West frequently wound up on *skid row.*

It may be a surprise to learn that this term, now generally associated with Manhattan's Bowery or some other urban slum, is of Western origin. It comes from the logging camps, and the original version was *skid road*. Walter McCulloch explains the variation from a slightly puristic bias:

> Careless reporters with dirt in their ears have written skid row or skidrow so often that this undesirable phoney term is accepted by the ignorant. There is no such damn thing as skidrow and never was.

In the early days of Northwestern lumbering, logs were skidded along a road in what is now called Yesler Way in Seattle. When the logging business became profitable, booze, women, and gambling became available to a logger, and the establishments needed for putting those operations under cover sprang up along the way.

Once *skid road* came to mean a collection of honky-tonks, bars, and cheap lodging houses, its logging associations ceased to be important. (Somewhat formally, we can say that the semantic feature, logging, was lost from the term's inventory.) The buildings were typically arranged in a row. Furthermore, 'road' and 'row' are similar in sound, and the term *skid* practically invites metaphorical interpretation. A drunken man may be closer to "skidding" than walking as he makes his way along the street.

The original log that went down skid road was *on the skids,* as a person going from respectability to skid row (or the gutter) might be. To facilitate the movement of the logs, loggers used to *grease the skids*. An 1893 citation from Oregon refers to the *skid-greaser,* who "lubricated the skids with oil so the logs would slide easily." Metaphorically, the term spread as far as the big Northern cities, in the sense of helping someone along the road to ruin, as, for example, by buying a drink for an alcoholic who was trying to reform.

The lumbering term has a predecessor, if not an ancestor, in nautical terminology: *greasing the way.* In a typically British development, this phrase acquired the more general sense of 'making preparations in advance to secure influence to get an appointment or the like'. The British and American expression *to grease the palm* 'bribe' is another development in the same complex of terms.

Eventually *skid row* lost the last splinter of its logging associations. In 1944, it was defined in a semiacademic journal, *Notes and Queries,* as 'a district of cheap flophouses, employment agencies, etc.' But strong associations with alcohol, alcoholism, and the barroom remain.

As we have seen, most dedicated drinkers of the West believed that, far from putting one on the skids, whiskey had some protective or medicinal value. The same faith was often expressed in the other minor vice to which Mrs. Trollope objected so vehemently, the use of tobacco. Texas scout Bigfoot Wallace is reported as having said:

> These [his boots] don't protect you against the stinging scorpions, 'cow-killers', and scaly-back cinches that crawl about at night when you are asleep! The only way to keep them at a distance is to 'chaw' tobacco and drink whiskey, and that is the reason the Temperance Society never flourished much in Texas.[16]

Most of the terms for tobacco came, obviously, from the East and the Indians, but the frontiersman added a few of his own. Maybe he got them from Indian tribes that the other colonists were not in contact with, like the Navaho whose *Zilth-Nut-to* 'mountain tobacco' was reported in 1938. The Western Indians' smoking material of willow bark, sometimes mixed with tobacco, was often called *killikinic* or *kinnikinic.*[17] Naturally the cowboy preferred *store tobacco,* first attested from *Huckleberry Finn* in 1884 and contrasted to the less desirable product, therein labeled *niggerhead.* The use of *store* in compounds is strikingly American: *store bill, store goods, store-bought* (first attested in Texas in 1853 but soon very widespread), *store boots, store candy, store cheese, store dress, store medicine, store pants, store sugar,* and *store teeth.* Most of these phrases are first attested between 1851 and 1898.

The way of the West was not, however, to smoke machine-rolled cigarettes but to *roll one's own.* This phrase is not attested in *The Dictionary of Americanisms* before 1913, but there is very good reason to suspect that it is older than that. A 1923 citation from Clarence E. Mulford's *Hopalong Cassidy,* a rather good fictional representation of Western matters, sets the phrase at least fictionally a great deal earlier. Since Wister's *Journal* of the 1890's, among many other sources, refers constantly to smoking, and since machine-rolled cigarettes would not have been available, it is very likely that the cowboy was "rolling his own" by that time.

Rolling the cigarette with one hand, because the other was needed to hold the reins, was a well-known test of cowboy ability. In the early twentieth century, the most used brands of tobacco for "makings" were Bull Durham, which came to be a kind of symbol for cheap materials, and Duke's Mixture, which was proverbial in the same sense that Heinz was later. Thus a dog was a "Duke's Mixture" if its ancestry was very patently mixed, just as it subsequently was called "Heinz" (fifty-seven varieties). Those able to afford the better things could have *ready rolls,* not even mentioned in any of the dictionaries but widely current in Texas by the 1920's. The *corncob pipe* (1829) was more characteristic of the farmer than of the cowboy or the Westerner.

What Mrs. Trollope saw as ravaging the health of the nonliterary American was chewing tobacco rather than anything smoked. *Plug tobacco,* the variety used for a "chaw," goes back to 1814; *chewing tobacco* itself, to 1789, in Boston. It is also attested from Virginia in 1835 and from Ardmore, Oklahoma, in 1948, and, as everyone knows, was in all sorts of other places between and after those dates. *Chaw tobacco,* considered obsolete by *A Dictionary of Americanisms,* had a vogue from Kentucky to California between 1834 and 1858.

Taking tobacco directly into the mouth had a greater "kick," and was popular among those who really enjoyed the effects of nicotine. A cowboy proverb, developed from self-confident talk to a horse one was trying to break, was "The higher you pitch, the sweeter my Navy tastes." *Navy* is short for *Navy plug,* attested as early as 1876. It was also a brand name for chewing tobacco; a successor in the twentieth century was *Star Navy.* In the early 1920's, a tobacco chewer might boast that he could "Chew Star Navy and spit ham gravy," referring of course to the color of the stream he spat forth. Contemporary plug tobacco brand names run to plain ones like *Day's Work, Brown Mule,* and *Red Man;* but in 1837, Captain Frederick Marryat referred to a brand with the Latinate name of *Dulcissimus,* and Mrs. Trollope cited the almost equally elegant *Celebrated Chewing Tobacco.*

Given the potency of the plug tobacco, it was a real problem for the chewer to avoid *biting off more than he could chew,* a phrase still used for taking on something beyond one's capabilities. *Chaw* rather than *chew* was the form recorded in the first attestation of the phrase, in Beadle's *Western Wilds and the Men Who Redeem Them* (1878). The term, with that meaning, is quite obviously Western in origin. There was an Eastern predecessor— *bite off,* meaning 'shut up'—but there could hardly be any connection between the two.

Elsewhere in the United States, the practice of *dipping snuff* was widespread, the term being first recorded in

1848. (It is probably much older, however; the practice itself was observed by Columbus's men among the Carib Indians on Cuba.) Early observers placed it in Virginia and North Carolina; others called it Southern in general, and it is true that [W. E. "Levi"] *Garrett's Snuff, Honest Snuff,* and *Red Rooster Snuff,* among other brands, had their most devoted customers in the Southern and Southwestern states. A straw or twig was dipped into the snuff box to remove the tobacco product, which was then transferred to the lower lip. The "toothbrush" (so called by old women in Texas in the 1930's) was also used to stir the snuff around to the most advantageous locations so that its full narcotic power might be realized.

Women were more addicted to this vice than men. A tempting explanation, casually arrived at, would be that until the twentieth century it was considered shocking for women to smoke. However, Josiah Gregg's 1844 *Commerce of the Prairies* tells us that, in the Southwest at least, cigarette smoking was "a habit of which the loveliest and most refined equally partake."[18]

The American frontier had little use for the delicate snuffboxes Europeans and some Easterners affected. They took the powerful narcotic the American Indians bequeathed to the world straight or rolled in cigarettes, and they took a lot of it. A great deal of the terminology they used reflects that consumption. *Up to snuff,* although not an Americanism in the narrow sense that the historical dictionaries first record its use here, is now regarded by Englishmen as an approximate American equivalent of *quite acceptable.*[19] Their perception may involve a reality more significant than mere historical primacy.

6

Nomadic Westerners: Mountain Men and Cowboys

Developing American phraseology, except for the early influence of the Six Nations of the Iroquois, came primarily from the West. As the frontier moved, and the population moved with it, the language changed. (To say that it "grew" is to risk inaccuracy, since it is possible that for every expression "added" another was "lost.") It would be oversimplification, however, to present the picture as one continuous westward movement. A lot of the pioneers turned back, and some of the travelers made plans to return before they even started west. Others were nomadic, like the trappers and the cowboys. As much as any other interlocutors, they dealt with the Western Indians; and, according to those who have represented their speech, they either learned the Indians' language (especially if they lived with a tribe for a time) or used Pidgin English with them. Both practices had important linguistic consequences.

The advance group in the Far West was the trappers, or mountain men, who flourished between 1810 and 1840. We are fortunate to have excellent literary descriptions of them and representations of the talk of actual trappers like Old Bill Williams and James P. Beckwourth. Their speech is an important indicator of what was happening to American English on the frontier in the nineteenth century.

They further bear out what Captain Marryat recorded about the "jargon" formation of Americans:

> The Americans . . . borrow their similes very much from the nature of their occupations and pursuits.[1]

They also exemplify the effects on the vocabularies of occupational groups of dealing with speakers of other languages

In addition to common Westernisms like *savvy* and *palaver* (ultimately from Pidgin English) and the general intensifier *heap,* the mountain man's vocabulary reflected his business. Since the beaver was his staple pelt, he felt it appropriate to carry over the term for remuneration that had been used earlier in the Eastern states. For the Eastern trapper who was having trouble getting pelts, the attraction of the Rockies "running over with beaver" was irresistible.[2] Obviously, he carried his trade language along with him; but it changed in transit.

When the mountain man asked, "Whose beaver you earnin'?" meaning 'Who are you working for?' or 'Who's paying you?' he was carrying on the trapper's tradition reflected in the promise to pay four men "by giving them two hundred beavers" recorded in Massachusetts in 1721.[3] In the colonial period, *beaver pay,* which came from the Dutch, meant 'payment in beaver, or at the value of it'. The Jamaica, Long Island, *Record* for 1662 reports how some people "are to pay twentie three pounds in bever pay"[4]; and the New Jersey Archives for 1685 record the "disbursement of four pounds a peice [sic] in bever pay."[5] Canadian trappers in Montreal had their Beaver Club, on Beaver Hill, to be eligible for which one had to spend at least one winter at the trapper's trade.[6] The pull of the beaver terminology was apparently so great that it at least partially reversed the general trend of maritime influence:

the first steamship on the Pacific side, flagship of the Hudson's Bay Company, was known as the *Beaver*.[7]

The spin-off from beaver-trapping terminology was tremendous, although the relationship is not always obvious to those who have not studied the records of the trapper's life. If the beaver swam away with a trap, for example, all was not lost—there was a *float stick* (Adams, in *Western Words*, uses the even more picturesque term *float-my-stick*) attached which would tell where the trap had gone. From this, mountain men came to use *the way the stick floats* for 'what's up' or 'what's what'. This usage preceded the rough equivalents used by later groups, which expressed a more coddled way of life: *the way the ball bounces, the way the cards are stacked,* and even *the way the cookie crumbles.*

Mountain men may not have been the first to use the beaver figuratively, but someone made *eager beaver* and *work like a beaver* familiar terms, and there are no better candidates for the honor. Trappers made noteworthy adaptations of the term. When they were gambling, they often said, "Ho, boys! Hyar's a deck, and hyar's the beaver!" meanwhile rattling the coin that served as stake in the game.[8] A trapper with alcoholic supplies might greet a friend with "Worth a pack of beaver to see you, you old bastard, and if you got a dry, here's whiskey."[9] The term *dry,* associated with the lack of alcoholic drink, had been of very long use in England, but primarily as an adjective; the U.S. system of voting precincts "wet" or "dry" and designation of people favoring one ticket or the other as *wets* or *dries* was well in the future. The mountain man was thus somewhat innovative grammatically in using *dry* as a noun.

The mountain man might relieve the monotony of collecting pelts and sitting out heavy snowfalls with whiskey and a deck of cards, but most of the time neither of these was available. "Yarning"—telling tales—was almost his only entertainment, and he developed a high degree of verbal inventiveness and a colorful vocabulary. Perhaps to avoid the monotony of using the first person singular, he commonly referred to himself as "this beaver," "this Injun," or "this hoss"—obviously terms from the most important aspects of his work and contacts. He might even refer to himself as "this coon" or "this nigger."

The use of what are now ethnic slur words is startling at first reading, but these words are everywhere in the records. Black men were important participants in the fur trade, as in other frontier occupations, and sometimes they were more successful than the white mountain men in dealing with the Indians. The Indians themselves took note of the color of the descendants of Africans and called them by terms like "little black white man" or *wassabajinga* 'little black bear'.

In gauging the significance of these terms, one must remember that even *nigger* was not offensive to Blacks until whites used it in a derogatory way. A. S. L. Adams' *Nigger to Nigger* (1928) could still use the term inoffensively. In Haitian Creole, *nég* (from French *négre*) means 'person' and can have a prestigious connotation (*Li gro neg* 'He's an important person'). Puerto Ricans often express solidarity by calling each other *Negro* or *Negra*—not always with reference to color. In the mountain man's speech, it was a way of fitting the simple first-person referent into a generally figurative way of talking:

Hyar's a niggur lifted hair [i.e., took a scalp] on that spree [in that battle].[10]

The mountain man's use of *nigger* and sometimes of *coon* may have been influenced by the practices of the minstrel shows back east. The latter term had had a long currency in American English, however. In 1839, Captain Marryat reported:

> In the Western states, where the racoon is plentiful, they use the abbreviation *coon* in speaking of people.[11]

For the mountain man, *some coon* or *some beaver* meant a trapper outstanding in some way; the terms had none of the racial offensiveness of "All coons look alike to me." A mountain man who fell ill, died, or fell in love was "a gone beaver" or "a gone coon" to his colleagues. The latter, if not the former, had a rather widespread currency among other groups.

If the trapper's misfortune was being killed, especially in a fight, his survivors might report that he had been *rubbed out*. Mencken thought that *to rub out* came from Prohibition gangster talk:

> In the days of Prohibition, the racketeers invented (or had invented for them by newspaper reporters) a number of picturesque terms for to kill . . . [including] *to rub out*.[12]

He traced the transmission confidently:

> A large part of the vocabulary of the rum-running mobs of Prohibition days passed into the general speech, e.g., *to rub out*.[13]

It may be that the general public learned *to rub out* from the Prohibition mobsters or from the newspaper stories and movies about them, but mountain men and Indian uses of the term antedate those of the "rum-runners" by more than fifty years. There is a record of Black Elk, an Oglala Sioux holy man, protesting in 1863 about how "the

Wasictus [white men] were coming and that they were going to take over our country and rub us all out."[14] In the same year, British traveler Richard Burton reported *rubbed out* 'extinct' in a Western context. The term is used in George Ruxton's *Life in the Far West* (published in 1848) and prominently featured in *Life and Adventures* (1856) by the Black frontiersman James P. Beckwourth, as well as in the biography of "Old Bill" Williams, who died in 1849. Ruxton's footnote in *Life in the Far West* derives the term from "the Indian figurative language." The Plains Indian sign language communicates *kill* by a kind of rubbing motion, and that may well be the source of the expression. The sign language also expresses *die* by moving one hand from above the other to below it. The mountain man's *go under* is clearly a verbalization of this sign.

If, instead of death, the trapper were merely the victim of love, he could be a gone beaver for a "punkin," an attractive Indian girl. (We still use "some punkins" for an attractive girl 127 years after Ruxton recorded it in *Life in the Far West*.) She wasn't Algonquian, of course, but Blackfoot, Sioux, Cheyenne, or even Digger; the term, however, fits the westward movement pattern in that *pumpkin* was first borrowed from Algonquian. (And *some pumkins* fits into a subtler and perhaps more basic pattern in that the expression moved from west to east.) The pretty young girl could also be described as a *fofarrow,* especially if she was delicate or put on airs. Philologist and folklorist Louise Pound has suggested that it was a kind of blend of French *frou frou* and Spanish *fanfarron,* a suggested origin that at least fits the basic meaning of the word, 'trinkets and finery'. That meaning is obviously intended in this speech from one of Ruxton's characters:

"First I had a Blackfoot [squaw]—the darndest slut as ever cried for fofarrow . . . There warn't enough scarlet cloth nor beads, nor vermillion in Sublette's packs for [another one of his squaws]. Traps wouldn't buy her all the fofarrow she wanted.[15]

According to Ruxton, a trapper like Killburn (the speaker above) had very direct methods of dealing with his conjugal problems: he traded the second squaw to a Swede named Cross-Eagle and "lodge-poled" (beat with the pole that supported the tent) the first. The Indians' type of housing, if not the Indians' practices in identical situations, obviously provided this term for disciplinary methods.

The trapper's life was subject to constant danger. His frequent going in and out of places and situations took him into heroic "sprees"—battles in which he might be alone or outnumbered by Indians. He was always in danger of being "raised" (robbed) of his "possibles" (clothes, kitchen utensils, etc.) by *freebooters*—another term from the Atlantic language contact situation that found its way west. (See Chapter 2.) If he encountered hostile Indians, he was "in a fix."

Part of his distinctive vocabulary also derived from his constant hunting for food. *To make meat* was to be successful in the hunt. If the hunting hadn't been so good recently, he might be *froze for meat* (longing for or ardently desirious of it). He hunted almost exclusively for *buffler,* buffalo. His hunting was greatly helped by the fact that his game was *buffler-witted* 'dim-witted'; the term could also be applied to other game or to human beings. A really dense hunter might not *know poor bull from fat cow* (in much the same way that later dunces were said not to know *which end is up, what the score is, how to tell their asses from holes in the ground. Fat cow* could refer to anything of high grade, because the female buffalo, except immediately after calving, was considered much more edible by the hunters of the Northwest. In

Louisiana, however, people used to swear that if the testicles of the bull were removed immediately after killing, the meat was better than that of any cow.

The diet of the trapper consisted almost entirely of meat. Besides buffalo, he might eat beef, rabbit, dog—when hunting was really bad—or "painter" (panther). Like the Indians and Louisianians, the trappers were fond of *boudins,* the buffalo's intestines, one of an appreciable number of French borrowings on the frontier. Lewis and Clark's account of their expedition reported the eating of what the cook called "the *boudin (poudinge) blanc.*"[16]

French entered into the trapper's language and environment almost as much as Spanish did into the cowboy's. Historian Bliss Isley believes that it is only by chance that we think of the mountain men as primarily English-speaking:

> The best-known of the mountain men were of American origin. This is due to the fact that when they returned to St. Louis to visit they were sought by newspaper writers, who published the stories of their adventures in the *St. Louis Republic* and other papers of the day. Since the reporters did not speak French, they did not interview the French-speaking trappers. Yet these Frenchmen have left us innumerable place names in the mountain states.[17]

One of those place names was that of the mountain—Grand Teton; the mountain men understood the phrase, and playfully translated it as *Titty Mountain.* The place for the annual meeting to exchange furs and provisions was called the *rendezvous*—not the first use of the term in English by any means; but the term could not have been learned by the trappers from the borrowing in 1591, which is the first English use reported by *The Oxford English Dictionary.*

On the plains, if not in the mountains, one of the most familiar trees was the *bois d'arc (Maclura pomifera),* so called because of the Indian use of its wood (*bois*) for a bow (*arc*). The pronunciation was Americanized, in vernacular use, to "bowdark." Lieutenant Colonel Richard Irving Dodge actually spelled it that way in *The Plains of the Great West* (circa 1874). The fruit of the bois d'arc was inelegantly called *horse apple,* reportedly because horses will eat it. On the plains, *bois de vache* 'cow chips' was the frequently used named for a convenient fuel—cow manure.

Ruxton derives *plews* 'beaver pelts' from the French *plus.*[18] The semantic association of the word for 'more' with another pelt seems reasonable enough, and the compound *beaverplew* 'beaver pelt' shows how completely the form was assimilated. The fact that beaver was used as currency led to sentences like the following from *Life in the Far West: A plew a plug,* '[chewing tobacco costs] one beaver pelt for one plug'. For 'free' the trapper used the phrase *on the peraira.* The last word, a mispronunciation of the French *prairie,* suggests that, in the mountains as in Louisiana, English speakers generally insisted on the dominance of their own language rather than learning the other fellow's well.

Among the trapper's many language contacts, his contact with the Indians, who frequently entered his life, was perhaps the most extensive. Exchange of vocabulary was facilitated by language contact solutions like the one described in *Life in the Far West*:

> . . . the Indian exclaimed in broken Spanish and English mixed, "*Si, si,* me Arapaho, white man *amigo.* Come to camp—eat heap *carne*—me *amigo* white man. Come from Pueblo—hunt Cibola—me gun break—*no puedo matar nada: mucha hambre* (very hungry)—heap eat.

In such a polyglot context, familiar words took on new meanings. *Medicine,* a term of power for the Indian, became the trapper's word for the musk he took from the glands of the beaver and used as a scent to attract the animal to his traps. The word entered into compounds like *medicine man, medicine animal, medicine arrow, medicine bag, medicine dance, medicine lodge, medicine hunt, medicine pouch, medicine song,* and *medicine stone,* as well as Medicine Hat, a place name in Canada. Features of the Indians' way of thinking had profound effects on some of the mountain men:

> They learned Indian skills . . . They learned Indian dances. Even the Indian medicine made more sense than white religion to a lot of them, and some of them adopted Indian religion.[19]

The mountain men's relations with the Indians, especially with the Blackfeet, were sometimes hostile; but more often they were friendly. Like other frontier groups, many trappers became *squaw men,* lovers of Indian women. Many others tangled with Indian men and were scalped. To celebrate their own victories, the mountain men scalped in their turn. The process was known as *raising* or *lifting hair.* One of Ruxton's characters boasts, "I've raised the hair of more than one Apache."[20] Although the relationship isn't immediately apparent, the mountain man's phrase for something done thoroughly, *up the Green River,* also has Indian-fighting associations: scalping knives were manufactured near the Green River.

Since he had little or no formal schooling, the mountain man's English would not have satisfied the purist. But from at least one point of view, he was a real virtuoso. His English was as far from British—either standard or "folk" speech—as any variety of the language aside from Pidgin or Creole could be. In that sense at least, he was the most "American" of speakers.

In the latter part of the nineteenth century, the trappers began to be pushed out by other groups with different life styles. A. B. Guthrie's *The Way West* contains an excellent, if fictional, description of the emotions thus aroused:

> He [Lije Evans, a mountain man employed as guide] didn't blame the Oregoners as he had known old mountain men to do. Everybody had his life to make and every time its way, one different from another. The fur hunter didn't have title to the mountains no matter if he did say finders keepers. By that system, the country belonged to the Indians, or maybe someone before them. No use to stand against the stream of change and time.[21]

After the trappers came wagon trains with farmers and families and plows, to dispossess rather than to mix with the Indians. Instead of tepees and lodges, they built *dugouts, sod shanties,* and (when their situations improved) *log cabins.* They were more businesslike and less fanciful than the mountain men, in language and otherwise. But there was another group, ranging from Texas up through Montana, that lasted somewhat longer and carried on the tradition of imaginative discourse. This was, of course, the cowboys.

The cowboys were never as close to the Indians as the mountain men had been. They did not live among them, hunt with them, or make the buffalo the staple of their diet, and there is little evidence that they were as likely to cohabit with Indian women on any permanent basis. But, especially on the trail, they had constant contacts with the red men, who sometimes developed a taste for beef and had to be bought off with the gift of a steer or two, and communication with Indians was a regular part of the cowboy's speech activity.

As a functional member of the polyglot frontier speech community, the cowboy could speak the frontier *lingua franca,* Pidgin English. In addition to *long time no see* and *no can do,* he would use a phrase like *no work, much eat* for a tramp. An occasional etymological puzzler like *cavort* ("The calf kicked and cavorted around") can plausibly be linked to the Romance-based Lingua Franca tradition which produced all the European-based pidgins and creoles. (See Chapter 1.) The form in that language, cited as the source by *The Oxford English Dictionary,* was *cavolta. Cavort* has been in use in American English, as a rough equivalent of *horsing around,* since 1830.

But the major European language with which the cowboys dealt was Spanish. Early Texans had to learn from the Mexicans how to handle long-horned cattle on the open range. In the process they picked up words like *rodeo,* the gathering of cattle to be branded into a circle. (On the open range, they were set to that circular movement called *milling* when it was necessary to avoid a *stampede,* another word from Spanish—*estampeda.*) *Rodeo* was such a basic concept that, when the range became basically monolingual and English-speaking, it was translated into *round-up,* which can be either a noun or a verb. *Rodeo* then came to mean an exhibition of cowboy skills.

Exposure to Spanish, and proficiency in it, varied greatly with different cowboy groups. In the early days, when Texans had a real need to be bilingual, their Spanish was, for obvious reasons, better than that of the cowboys who arrived after "Anglos" were dominant and felt free to express contempt for "Latins" or "greasers." Catch-as-catch-can translation resulted in redundancies like *gramma grass,* reported by British traveler Sir Richard Burton in 1860, which combines the Spanish word for grass, *grama,* with the English. Another such doublet was *lover wolf,* an expression generated not by any sexual connotations but by folk-etymological associations with the Spanish word for wolf, *lobo.* Owen Wister, who reported that form, also recorded *loafer* as a garbled version of *lobo*. The Westerner's version of Spanish could be as phonologically near-accurate as *hoosegow* from *juzgado* (dropping the *d* from the final syllable as most Mexican and Latin American speakers do) or as distorted as *wrangler* from *caballerangero*. The latter was often part of the half-translated compound *horse wrangler*. Another such compound was *cowboy* itself: Spanish *vaquero* is composed of a combining form of the word for *cow* (*vaca*) and an agent suffix.

A primary activity of the round-up was *branding* the cattle. The term meant burning a design symbolic of a given ranch or owner into the hide of the cow—from a cognate with *burn*. (See the discussion of *brandy* in Chapter 5.) *Brand,* meaning a fire, had been in use in British English since 1400; but both *brand* (noun) and *brand* (verb) applied specifically to cattle are Americanisms. The attestations indicate that only the noun is of Western origin (Texas, in 1834); the verb is attested in Connecticut in 1634.

Brands had to be original and were often picturesque, but it is not true that the design of a bar followed by a *B* and a *Q,* the brand of a ranch famous for its way of roasting beef, was the origin of the word *barbecue*. On the contrary, the word comes from a Carib Indian word (variously transcribed as *barbacòa* or *babracot* by early French travelers in the Caribbean) and was transmitted to Spanish before it ever came to English.

Rather than rope a calf, the cowboy might *bulldog* it. This action consisted of the cowboy's jumping from the back of his horse and grasping the cow by the head, twisting its neck, and flipping it over on the ground, an action that in no way suggests a bulldog. However, we learn from biographer Esse F. O'Brien's *The First Bulldogger* that the Black cowboy Bill Pickett, when he performed such an action, used to sink his teeth into the steer's tender nose. Apparently the term that described Pickett's performance was transferred to a less sensational method.

An unbranded steer or calf with an ear mark (a design cut into the animal's ear to designate ownership) was called a *sleeper*. *The Oxford English Dictionary* gives the first occurrence of the term as 1910, but Owen Wister used it in 1893. An entry in the *OED* for a 1918 occurrence suggests that a "sleeper" might be 'something taken for something else'. In that sense, it may well be the source for our present usage meaning a play (or movie, book, athlete, or politician) that unexpectedly achieves great success. Another show-business term, a *stinker*, may also be borrowed from Westerners. Among buffalo hunters, an unskilled hand would be given the repulsive task of skinning the freshly killed animal. Because of the blood, intestines, and other parts of the buffalo that adhered to the skinner, he was an obvious "stinker." The extended usage takes off from this meaning of a strong smell, but it later acquired other (perhaps stronger) associations of selfishness, untrustworthiness, etc.

A cow or calf that had no brand and could be claimed by anyone was known as a *maverick*, from the family name of a prominent rancher in Texas who either lost a lot of cattle because he refused to brand his own or gained a lot because he had a propensity for latching on to the unbranded property of others, depending upon which legend you believe. The term is widely used today for a nonconformist, especially in politics.

More of a mystery is the term *dogie* for a motherless calf. In the metaphorical sense of 'waif', the term has had a distribution as far north as Canada. The first recorded occurrence, from *Century Magazine* for 1888, reflects the general puzzlement about the term:

A bunch of steers had been traveling over the scoria buttes to the head of Elk Creek; they were mostly Texas doughies—a name I have never seen written but it applies to young immigrant cattle.

Linguists may tend to sneer at the writer's concern about "a name written," but spellings often reflect a theory about the origin of a word. *The Dictionary of Canadianisms* is apparently influenced by such evidence in deriving the word from *dough-guts* "with reference to a bloated belly resulting from poor feeding"; evidence from the 1890's, however, makes the term a synonym for "barnyard cattle," which are hardly ill-fed compared to range cattle. The wild guess that *dogie* represented a clipped (and distorted) form of Spanish *adobe* 'mud' is even worse than the other suggestion.

In 1893, Owen Wister recorded a version of a cowboy folk song still well known:

Sing hooplio get along my little dogies,
For Wyoming shall be your new home.
Its [sic] hooping and yelling and cursing these dogies
To our misfortune and none of your own.[22]

Wister elsewhere recorded the use of *doga* to mean "anything in stock that's trifling', thus providing the only known hint about another form of the word.[23] It must be remembered that dogies are small. "Git along, *big* dogies," would be unthinkable.

Under the circumstances, an African origin of *dogie* cannot be ruled out entirely. It is certainly more likely than spontaneous generation by an anonymous Texas cattleman, as Adams suggests in *Western Words*. There were many Black cowboys in the West, and more Afro-English influence on the language than has so far been generally admitted.[24] Linguist Julian Mason, for example, convincingly compared *buckaroo* to the Gullah (and general Afro-English) *buckra,* upsetting the previously accepted derivation from Spanish *vaquero*.[25] Bantu language cognates of Swahili *kidogo* 'a little', *-dogo* 'small', including Bambara *dogo* 'small, short', Gã *ateké* 'short', and Twi *ateké* 'short-legged', are as likely a source as anything suggested so far. Turner's *Africanisms in the Gullah Dialect* (1949) attests the use of *Dogo* as a personal name and cites the Bambara form as a possible source. The *Dictionary of Jamaican English* lists *dogi* 'short, small' and the typically Afro-Creole iterative *dogi dogi*. It also attests Jamaican compounds like *dogi fowl* 'a small fowl', *dogi hen* 'a small hen', and *dogi man* 'a short man'. The last is directly paralleled by *dogieman* in *Western Words*, which also lists the compound *dogie lamb*.

Rustler is the word for what became the major threat to the cattle industry once the trail hands had learned to deal with the Indians. *The Oxford English Dictionary* lists it from 1882, from *Blackwood's Magazine*, but with a clear American reference:

> a gang of "rustlers"—as the lawless desperadoes who
> abound in Arizona, New Mexico, and Texas are called . . .

The term is so familiar, in this meaning, from Western writings that the early Americanism meaning 'an energetic or bustling man' has been driven out of currency. It apparently survived for a while among other Western groups, however; Scotty, the miner in Mark Twain's "Buck Fanshaw's Funeral," eulogizes his departed friend with "But pard, he was a rustler." Owen Wister, in 1893, commented upon the great problem produced by cattle-stealing ("about three years ago this part of the country was in a high state of disorder") and gave a picturesque local definition of *rustler:* 'eating too much beef without owning cattle'.[26] Apparently the very seriousness of the problem expedited the change from the Eastern meaning to the Western one, at least in cow country.

As the most important source of income for those parts of the West not lucky enough to have gold or silver, the cow was the formative element in a great deal of the terminology used in the area. The word *cowboy* did not itself originate in the United States; but the British usage (hyphenated *cow-boy,* as no red-blooded Westerner would ever write it), used as far back as 1725, meant 'a boy who tends cattle'. It took the American West to give it the meaning 'a man employed to take care of cattle on a ranch' —not only seeing that they had grass and water and keeping the flies away, but also roping and branding them, moving them thousands of miles over the cattle trails, and fighting against enemies of a sort hardly dreamed of in England. It took Western novels and movies to give the term the additional connotations of 'gunslinger' and a man fatally attractive to beautiful girls but with room in his affections only for his horse. The Dallas football team is now famous as the Cowboys; in a more innocent age, the Dallas Texas League baseball team was the Steers, a name totally inappropriate to the present era of *Playboy, Penthouse,* and porno movies, and one the population of Dallas would probably like to forget.

The element *-boy* has aroused the ire of the terminologically finicky, leading to a preference for *cowman* in some circles, but *cowboy* was not an opprobrious designation in the mid-nineteenth century. In those days, *firemen* were *fireboys* (*b'hoys* or even *bo'hoys* in the popular Broadway series about "Mose the Bowery B'hoy") even in New York City. *Boy* to designate a worker has figured in nautical usage since at least as early as Columbus' use of Spanish *muchacho* in that meaning in his diary of the discovery of the New World. And probably no one has yet thought of using the neologism *cowperson.*

Cowgirl, which also originated in England, has undergone an equal change. In England, it meant 'a girl who tends cows'; in the American West it came to mean 'feminine equivalent of cowboy' or even (as sentimentally sung by Dale Evans) 'a cowboy's sweetheart'.

Of the compounds with *cow* that developed in America before the Western ranches got going, only those most adapted to the business of the ranges were widely used. *Cow brute* was a euphemism for *bull* in the East but meant 'a wild cow, difficult to manage' on the ranches. *Cow path* and *cow pen* were both originally American but not Western, neither being a part of taking care of stock on the open range. *Cowkeeper* (1619) 'a person employed to look after the cows of a village' obviously had no place in the large-scale cattle business of the West. Cattle roam freely without fences in the Old West, and their paths were wide trails like the Old Chisholm Trail. *Cow town,* on the other hand, fits the scale of the Western cattle trade and originated in that area, dating from 1888. For many years, it has been the newspaper writer's pet name for Forth Worth, Texas, just as Motor City (or, now, Motown) has been for Detroit and The Windy City for Chicago. *Cowhide,* both the noun meaning 'a hand-whip' (1818) and the verb meaning 'to use same' (1820) are Americanisms. Although not necessarily Westernisms to begin with, they fit into the life style of the West and became naturalized there.

The railroad and the ranches frequently argued over the right of way, which may be one reason why public sympathies often went to Western outlaws (like Jesse James) who robbed the trains. *Cow-remover* (1848) was the original term for the railroad's attempt to cope with cattle that mistook the tracks for the range. Anyone who fails to understand why *cowcatcher* is more appropriate to the Western idiom has probably stopped reading before this point, anyway. In 1838, it was *cow- or horse-remover.* Around 1883, *cow-whistle* was used for the device with which the engineer tried to scare cows off the track. *Cow-bug* was in use from 1880 to mean a species of black beetle with yellowish spots on its back; *cow-killer* was a type of ant.

None of these is terribly important to the Western variety of English, and only *cowcatcher* found any general acceptance in American English. A mid-twentieth-century commentator on the political scene characterized the three- or four-minute speeches by minor local candidates that were tacked on to the President's speeches as "cowcatchers on the Prexy's talks."[27]

The cow country had its *cow camps* (1885) and *cow hands* (1886). *Hands,* as a designation for workers, has obvious nautical parallels, like many other Western terms. *Cowboy song* designates a very specific type of ballad, although the term seems to be missing from the historical dictionaries. Jack Thorp's *Songs of the Cowboys* was printed in 1908, and the compound itself could probably be quite easily found at an earlier date. *Cow pony* is first attested in 1874.

Each cowboy had five or six ponies assigned to him by the foreman: circle horses, roping horses, cutting horses, a night horse, and one or two broncos. Together they constituted his *string.* To lose one was a great misfortune, and to be deprived of one by the boss was the worst possible insult. Either eventuality constituted *breaking the string,* a very bad omen. Today *breaking a string* may mean losing a game after a series of victories, (e.g., to baseball players, who are highly superstitious about such matters). The dissociation of the phrase from the cattle trade may have been influenced by Western fiction, in which each cowboy has only one pure-white horse that is fanatically devoted to him and capable of running for miles at top speed in pursuit of the bad guys. Roy Rogers needed only Trigger, and a nation of movie watchers associated *string* with activities in which horses did not participate.

Being mounted on a good cow pony was sometimes a guarantee of survival even if the rider became incapacitated, since a good pony could find its way home without guidance. It could also do a great deal of the work of herding cattle without direct instructions from its rider. The term *horse sense* was beautifully descriptive of the mount's intelligence. *The Nation* for August 18, 1870, documented how the term, meaning 'plain, practical good sense,' had arisen in the West. It is significant that *horse sense* comes from the American West, but *horse play* and *horse laugh,* two terms with connotations unfavorable to the horse, do not. *Horsing around,* 'having things besides the business at hand on one's mind', is also not necessarily Western.

The cowboy's second most prized possession after his horse was his saddle. A man suspected of having a distorted sense of values could be stigmatized as owning "a five-dollar horse and a fifty-dollar saddle." The saddle, whatever its cost, was one of two types: a *stock saddle* or a *range saddle.* The latter, distinguished by the horn which was useful in roping, came originally from Africa by way of Spain via the Moors in the Middle Ages and then via the Spaniards to the New World, where it became known as a *cow saddle,* since it was useful in herding. If a cowboy lost his place in the profession completely, he was said to have *sold his saddle.* If he was a poor rider, he might *hunt leather,* hold on by the saddle horn or some other strap or string. An experienced cowboy, in Arizona anyway, knew how to *uncork a horse* 'ride a bucking horse until it bucked itself into submission'.

A rider who fell off *hunted dirt* (or *grass*), an expression that spread far beyond the cattle business. By the testimony of Mark Twain's writing, it reached the vocabulary of that other Western group of nomads in the mining camps. In "Buck Fanshaw's Funeral," Scotty says, describing his struggle to understand the parson's talk in terms of a fight, "When you get in with your left, I hunt grass every time." The seemingly related *bite the dust,* used in innumerable Western novels to describe the shooting down of a mounted Indian, is first recorded in a translation of—of all things—the *Iliad*. The translator was, however, the American poet William Cullen Bryant.

The records of Western usage reveal a great deal about the origin of American phraseology and suggest even more. Many of the phrases are not ones we would automatically trace back to the cattle business. *Like getting money from home* has a collegiate ring to it, but Wister called it Western in 1893. In this connection, one must remember that cow-punching was mainly a young man's profession, and a lot of those attracted to it may have been runaways or adventure-seekers who occasionally received money from their parents. Wister also attributed *hot in* (to most of us, *under*) *the collar* 'angry' to cowboy and Western usage. The background of this term is easy to understand if we remember the bandanna that formed a regular part of the cowboy's costume.

Most of us know *chuck*, the cowboy's term for food, and *chuck wagon*, the indispensable food-producing part of the retinue of the trail herd. However, few of even the unemployed among us today use the term *riding the chuck line* for 'being between jobs'.

Given his influence in bringing Mexican-Spanish words (*mañana, pronto, canyon, mesa, remuda, riata,* even *mecate* 'hair rope' in the form *McCarty*) into American English along with some of the phrases discussed above, the cowboy had an influence on the American vocabulary disproportionate to his numbers. In the dime novels of the nineteenth century and in the movies of the early and mid twentieth, the cowboy and the frontiersman were overexposed, and it became all too easy to assume that the works of the Western novelists were as phony as the endless television series about Davy Crockett, Wyatt Earp, and the earliest of all, Hopalong Cassidy. We may doubt the authenticity of the William Boyd portrayal of Cassidy, but the august *Oxford English Dictionary* cites from the

novels of C. J. Mulford, Cassidy's creator. Like Owen
Wister, he contributed to the vast corpus of reasonably
well authenticated Western speech that still awaits the
serious research of language historians.[28] Even the works
of Easterners like Max Brand and Zane Grey, a New York
dentist who knew little or nothing about the West at first
hand, could make important contributions to our understanding of how Western phrases became part of the general American vocabulary.

Colorful as they were, the trappers and the cowboys were
only two groups of nomadic Westerners. There were also
miners, lumberjacks, stagecoach riders, paying and non-
paying passengers on railway trains, and many others.
Each group had its vocabulary or occupational "jargon."[29]
For reasons peculiar to my own research and reading interests, I have chosen to illustrate the point about Western
vocabulary by the cowboys and the mountain men. The
thesis that a substantial amount of the American lexicon
originated in the West and then moved East, against the
pattern of migrating farmers, can be supported just as
well, however, by other groups.

In logging, for example, to *drag one's feet* was to ride
the (two-man) saw and fail to do one's share. For Americans today, the phrase means 'fail to do one's part in any
cooperative enterprise', and more than two persons can
be involved. In the logging camps a *back log* was an im-
mense log against which the fire was built. Metaphorically
applied, the phrase came to mean anything held in reserve
and then later 'unfilled orders'. Today a housing con-
tractor might have a "backlog" of orders for artificial
fireplaces.

Miners seem to have contributed even more to the inventory of American phrases. From the Gold Rush of
1849 we got *prospector* (1851) and phrases like *strike it rich*
(1852). *Pan out* 'be successful' meant, in 1851, 'to obtain
gold by washing ore in a miner's grub pan'; by 1873, it

had the general sense it has today. *Stake a claim* referred to the process of establishing one's exclusive rights to a potentially rich piece of mining land, and a *claim jumper* was one who ignored the marking of such rights. Today, the former phrase could apply to giving a girl an engagement ring, and the latter to someone else who dated her anyway. A person with a successful (mining) claim might *make a stake* 'earn some money, make a fortune'. If his prospects of doing so were good, a wealthy nonprospector might *grubstake* him—advance the money needed for his living expenses in exchange for a share of the eventual strike. Of course, even pay dirt would *peter out* after a time.

There is much overlapping in the usages of these essentially nomadic groups, and it is risky to say dogmatically that a term came "originally" from one group or the other. There were no lexicographers in the logging and mining camps, and the first attestations we have were written down after the words and phrases had been in daily use for a period of years. Mencken (Supplement II, p. 761) points out how a word like *tenderfoot*, first used by cowboys for a cow new to the range, was popularized by miners. Walter McCulloch and Ramon Adams may claim the same phrase for the loggers and the cowboys, respectively, and my approach has been to conclude that both are probably right.

The interactions of the nomadic groups produce some fascinating possibilities for the future language historian. For example, there is the term *stiff* 'person, hobo' used by those who rode the freight trains during the Depression. It entered into many compounds, like *mission stiff* 'parson'. But the original usage was apparently on the Western ranches in the 1870's. There is some evidence that *stiff*, in this sense only, is a phonological variant of *stuff* (compare the way a young Northerner and an old-fashioned Southerner pronounce the second syllables of *Alice* and *Dallas*). *Stiff* in this sense meant 'corpse', and the *stiff man* on the ranches was the hand who disposed of carcasses by burning them. To call a man a *stiff* was to suggest that he had little worth, and the humorists of the hobo jungles found it an appropriate term. A tramp carrying his belongings over his shoulder in a bundle tied to a stick was a *bindle* (phonological variant of *bundle*, as with *stiff* and *stuff*) *stiff*, and a certain kind of cow was *brindle stuff*.[30]

There is too much of this for one book and one man. Others may find more complete and more satisfactory explanations; they may find groups even more fascinating than the cowboys and the mountain men. I have stuck to them because of my admiration for such guides as George Ruxton, Ramon Adams, and Philip Ashton Rollins. But it seems safe to say that whoever works with the Western territory and nomadic groups again will not find an exclusive pattern of Eastern words moving west.

7
Color Our
Talk Black

The mountain men and the cowboys were typically American in being mobile. Their opposites, the farmers and sheepherders, stayed put. The Blacks, whose influence on American English has been considerable, belonged to both groups. They produced fur traders like Jim Beckwourth and cowboys like Bill Pickett. As slaves on the Southern plantations, they also constituted the group most tied to one spot. It was not until the migrations to Northern cities after World War I that they joined to any great extent in the pattern of American mobility. That migration is famous because it included the movement of New Orleans jazzmen up the Mississippi to Chicago and then to New York. The second great exodus came during and just after World War II.

As the playmates of Southern white youngsters in pre–Civil War days, Blacks imparted a great deal of their own dialect to the white population, and words like *goobers* 'peanuts', *juke* 'a house of ill repute', *jazz* 'frenetic activity (basically associated with music)' became basic parts of American English. *Cooter* 'turtle' is known to whites in South Carolina, Georgia, and Mississippi; the Africanism *buckra* 'white man' means 'poor white trash' to even more residents of the Deep South. *Geechee*, used as a virtual synonym for *Gullah* on the Sea Islands of South Carolina and Georgia, means 'typically Black' to the Negro community on Cape Cod and 'mulatto' to the whites of north-western Louisiana. But the Blacks' primary contribution is the compounds they made out of familiar words.

As far as we can judge from historical documentation, the Negro on the Southern plantation—and, in the seventeenth and eighteenth centuries, on many Northern ones too—spoke a special variety of English that linguists would call a Creole—that is, a pidgin that has become the first, or only, language of a population group. Many attestations represent Blacks on the Southern plantations saying things like:

> boccarrora make de black man workee, make de horse workee, make ebery ting workee; only de hog. He, de hog, no workee; he eat, he drink, he walk about . . . he lib like a gentleman.[1]

This Creole variety of English was analogous to the variety of Dutch spoken in New York–New Jersey (Chapter 2) and to the "Gombo" variety of French spoken in Louisiana (see Chapter 3). It has gradually changed in the direction of Standard English (become decreolized) as the Black group has been acculturated, slowly, into the American mainstream; but just as the process of acculturation has not been completed, neither has the decreolization.

By the 1920's, the sophisticated adult Black male of Harlem was better known for this kind of talk than for pidgin:

> She laid the twister to her slammer on me, ole man, understand, and I dug the jive straight up and down, three ways sides and flats.

This seems to have nothing whatsoever in common with the pidgin quoted above, except perhaps for the comment of its author Dan Burley:

Such jargon is reminiscent of Tibet, Afghanistan, as unintelligible to the uninitiate as listening to a foreign dictator's harangue over a shortwave broadcast.[2]

Here's our old friend *jargon* again—just what everybody called Pidgin English, whether spoken by Chinese, Indians, or Blacks.

But it would be wasteful to go to Tibet or Afghanistan to find an analogue to this kind of "jargon." It would be cheaper, and more relevant, to go to Trinidad and listen to a couple of tesses limin' Old Talk—that is, to a couple of hip chicks from Trinidad talking the way they talk among their peers:

Jane: Nuh, man. You jokin. She horn he till de mark buss. Then he buss lash in she licks like fire and she buss durt. She friennin wid Johnny now.[3]

Many Harlemites would look down on the Trinidadians, but there is more in common between the speech of the two groups than meets the untutored eye or ear. The history—especially the early history—of English in Trinidad (or in Jamaica or any of dozens of other islands) is strikingly like that of Black English in the United States. Furthermore, even "jive talk" phrases like *play it cool* 'take it easy' or the ubiquitous term of address *man*[4] are as well known in Trinidad as in Harlem. There is perhaps a greater concentration of "jargon" phrases in the conversation imagined by Burley than in that by Otley, but this may be a matter of greater contrivance on the part of the former.

Like the slaves on the Caribbean islands, the slaves in the plantation South found it necessary to use a code vocabulary in order to conceal certain messages from their masters. (For historical reasons too complex to go into here, African languages were no longer available for such disguise purposes.)[5] Because religious meetings were tolerated

more extensively than other slave assemblies, the disguised
messages were most often transmitted through the medium
of religious songs ("spirituals"). Although the white
masters thought the "darkies" were expressing simple
religious devotion, they were actually conveying invitations to the meetings of an African cult of liberation.[6]
Steal away to Jesus was a code phrase amounting to an
invitation to a meeting of the cult.[7] *Judgment Day* was the
day on which the revolt was scheduled to take place.[8]
Jerusalem was Courtland, Southampton County, Virginia,
where revolt leader Nat Turner was incarcerated after his
capture. "Home," "Canaan," and "heb'm" were veiled
allusions to Africa, in some cases specifically Liberia.[9] A
song about a brother "a-gwine to Glory" referred to one
who had successfully boarded a repatriation ship.[10] An
occasional white church dignitary found out that "the
spiritual singing of the Negroes was according to the
African cult,"[11] but the disguise worked remarkably well.
However, after Turner's forces proved unequal to the
gigantic task they had undertaken, the double meanings
of the spirituals lost their force, and for some they came to
express truly pious sentiments. But the tradition of double
(or even multiple) meanings remained alive a long
time, for at least some members of the Black community.
And, as is well known, Black militancy, even after it had
lost its back-to-Africa emphasis, remained close to religion,
whether to a Christian sect, a Muslim group, or some more
exotic faith. The concept of *soul*, combining as it does the
Black protest movement with religious spirituality, would
have been impossible if historical conditions had been
different.

It is not certain that this tradition of disguise language
arose simply as a reaction to the challenge of the slave
environment or in the service of the African cult. There
have been long traditions of allusiveness and disguise
communication in African cultures.[12]

Part of this hidden usage results, as Karl Reisman has shown conclusively for Antigua, from ambivalence in the face of prejudice on the part of the "upper" white culture. When a mainstream culture deprecates his traditional values, the Black has often adopted that culture's disapproving terminology (on the surface) but given it his own meaning. Reisman has shown that *ugly* 'Afroid in facial features' is virtually the same as *beautiful,* given the proper context, for Antiguans. Since non-European things would be "bad," the most characteristically African traits of Black culture would be "bad"—but the Black felt a certain attraction for them anyway. *Bad* (especially when pronounced *ba-a-ad*) can mean 'very good, extremely good'. In such a context, *That woman is a bitch* is extremely complimentary, as is *She a tough bitch.* Dalby cites "frequent use of negative forms (often pronounced emphatically) to describe positive extremes in African languages."[13] And Black American linguist Grace Holt Sims calls the process "using The Man's language against him as a defense against sub-human categorization."[14]

For reasons like these, Black talk can frequently be misunderstood. *Mean* can carry the sense 'excellent'; Mean Joe Green, the defensive tackle for pro football's Pittsburgh Steelers, is mean in both senses—a defensive lineman has to love to hit running backs hard in order to be good at his job. *Uptight* is one of the most expressive of these chameleon words. It may mean either 'attractive, good' or 'unattractive, bad'. Early jazzmen associated it with preparedness: "I got my boots laced up tight (and am, supposedly, ready to go places)." Of course, too much preparedness could easily ruin the spontaneity needed for a jazz performance. A person who has his evening planned too exactly, who refuses to improvise with the group, is really "uptight."

Both *hot* and *cool* participate in this reversal. In the 1950's, jazzmen decided that being too *hot* 'frenetic, overactive' had left them open to exploitation, and *cool* 'detachment, ability to gauge the situation before acting' came to be the appropriate term. But coolness could go too far, as in Don Lee's fine poem about the Black who was so cool "he even stopped for green lights" and who failed to realize that in the end, "to be black is to be very-hot."

Some of the uses of *shit* within Black communication reflect the same kind of reversal. A successful pimp, a deejay who makes it, or any other person successful in the ways open to Blacks can be said to have *gotten his shit together*—that is, to have acted efficiently with regard to his most valuable (not least valuable) possessions or traits. Although the relationship between Black speakers and the drug trade is a two-way street,[15] and it is far from certain what the direction of influence has been unless there are clear-cut African or Creole analogues, the use of *shit* to mean 'heroin' (that is, something extremely costly, represented by something that can be had for less than nothing) probably represents a similar reversal.

Closely related to this reversal, and sometimes almost indistinguishable from it, is the use of indirection. Verbal games like *signifying, put-on, mocking the sender, doing the Tom Jones,* and *gamesmanship of Muhammad Ali* were examples of this kind of inversion:

> Blacks intentionally behave in ways which whites per-
> ceived as inappropriate but by which they were flattered,
> elevating "whitey" to a status they both knew he didn't
> occupy, invoking praise and ridicule in the same terms.
> The patrolman became a police "chief," the ex-private
> was elevated to "cap'n," the ex-captain to "colonel."[16]

Whether in terms of indirection or not, the plantation slave's need for a disguise language could take other forms than simply trying to fool the master concerning secret meetings. It could also be useful for communicating secret messages of a more personal nature:

Sometimes while loading corn in the field, which demands loud singing, Josh would call to Alice, a girl he wanted to court on the adjoining plantation, "I'm so hongry want a piece of bread"; and her reply would be "I'se so hongry almost dead." Then they would try to meet after dark in some secluded spot.[17]

The terminology of food—and especially of baked products —as disguised expressions for sexual intercourse is a strikingly pervasive theme in what little we have that can be considered reliable from the plantation literature and in jazz and blues lyrics. *Cookie, cake,* and *pie* are commonplace terms with this type of association; Guy B. Johnson reports that "in order to express superlatively his estimate of his sweetheart's sexual equipment, [the Black] often refers to it as *angel-food cake.*"[18] Harold Courlander, in *Negro Folk Music, U.S.A.*, attests the same meaning for *pie* and *custard pie.*[19] Johnson also reports the use of *bread* in that significance and postulates a "vulgar" second meaning for the title of the song "Short'nin' Bread":

One turned over [in bed] to the other an' said,
"My baby loves short'nin', short'nin' bread."[20]

If so, this would be a rather coarse, undistinguished kind of routine sex. *Corn bread* conveys the same meaning. *Biscuit,* on the other hand, betokens a finer product of baking and a more refined sexual experience. A *biscuit roller* is an especially talented lover, either male or female. Another blues song reports the wife who has "corn bread for her husband, biscuits for her backdoor man."[21]

The best known example of this kind of sexual disguise terminology, however, is *jelly roll.* In a real sense, this is an Africanism—or what is more significant in understanding Black Talk, the shaping of European material to an African pattern. David Dalby has shown that the term involves "Mandingo *jeli* 'minstrel' (often gaining popularity with women through his skill in the use of words and music)" and hypothesizes "convergence with English *jelly* and *jelly roll* (as items of food)."[22] Although the food reference may be dominant insofar as the white listener is concerned, Black texts show a fascinating awareness of both halves of the referential pattern:

> Jelly roll, jelly roll ain't so hard to find,
> There's a baker shop in town makes it brown like mine.
> I got a sweet jelly, a lovin' sweet jelly roll.
> If you taste my jelly it'll satisy your worried soul.[23]

> I ain't gonna give nobody none of this jelly roll.
> Nobody in town can bake sweet jelly roll like mine.
> Your jelly roll is good.[24]

The Southern whites' awareness of this meaning is shown by novels like Thomas Wolfe's 1929 *Look Homeward, Angel*. White characters used the term, although always referring to Black women. Newsboy Eugene Gant, trying to collect, has a memorable conversation with a Black customer who cannot pay:

> "I'll have somethin' fo' yuh, sho. I'se waitin' fo' a white gent'man now. He's gonna gib me a dollah." . . .
> "What's—what's he going to give you a dollar for?"
> "Jelly Roll."[25]

Within Afro-American culture, however, there is a deeper level to *jelly roll* than even Dalby has suspected. In the Caribbean, *jelly* is used to refer to the meat of the coconut in a still viscous stage. The *Dictionary of Jamaican English* reports the meaning 'an unripe cocoanut sold in the streets and the jelly eaten.' This meaning is cited as early as 1834; there are no known earlier attestations of the specifically Black meanings. To look at, this "jelly" closely resembles semen. A jelly roll, then, is, in one sense a (rock and) roll that produces jelly. From there, there is an easy transference—although there is no suggestion here that such was the historical process—to intercourse:

> Jelly, jelly, jelly; jelly stays on my mind,
> Jelly roll killed my pappy, it drove my mammy stone
>   blind.[26]

On a simple level, it is the woman whose contribution makes intercourse sweet, and the vagina, shaped like the bakery product, is the referent for *jelly roll*:

> Ain't been to hell but I been tol'
> Women in hell got sweet jelly roll.[27]

The truly hip male lover, however, knows how to make himself the more desirable one; he is a *sweet-back man*, and what he contributes becomes the jelly roll, which the female in her turn may long for:

> When your man comes home evil,
> Tells you you are gettin' old
> That's a true sign he's got someone else
> Bakin' his jelly roll.[28]

Like *rider* (as in both "Easy Rider" and "See, See, Rider") *jelly roll* is a bisexual (or, in more modern terms, unisexual) term. In the end, it simply means the process of intercourse, appreciated from the viewpoint of either female or male.

The hippest of the hip, the best of the jazzmen and the pimp, merited the name Jelly Roll. According to the biography by the late folklorist Alan Lomax, Ferdinand LeMenthe, who renamed himself Morton and made jazz history as leader of the Red Hot Peppers, inspired his nickname during a comedy performance onstage when the other Black comedian, using a pastry metaphor, proclaimed himself "Sweet Papa Cream Puff right out of the bakery shop." The only way Morton could top that one was to call himself "Sweet Papa Jelly Roll, with stovepipes in my hips and all the women in town dyin' to turn my damper down."[29] Lomax also makes it clear that prostitution was economically more important to Morton than music, enabling him to live the flashy life of a pimp and to wear diamond fillings in his teeth.[30]

The language of the pimp, besides being aggressively hip, is one of the more notable examples of trade jargon that couldn't help filtering out to square America. The prostitute's customer is no *sweetback man* or *sweet man*, but a *trick*, a term probably derived from nautical usage in the sense of 'a task',[31] or a *john* 'a dupe, someone to be deceived'.[32] With him, the prostitute will not *get her nut hot* 'become sexually stimulated' or *get her nut off* 'experience orgasm'. (In white terminology, *getting the nuts off* refers to the male orgasm exclusively.) A pimp prefers a woman who is *qualified* 'an experienced whore' but occasionally has to use a *turn out* 'a recently recruited prostitute'.[33] *Turn out* is another term adapted from nautical usage, where it is strictly a verb and means 'begin activity'. Its opposite, at sea, is *turn in* 'cease activity' or 'go to bed', a term that seems to have no special function among Black pimps and prostitutes.

Despite the familiarity of prostitution in the Black ghetto—or perhaps because of it—it plays an important role in the verbal insult ritual called *the dozens*:

At least my mother ain't no cake—everybody get a piece.[34]

The dozens is one of many ways in which the verbally superior ghetto male utilizes his superiority. Whether or not he intends to recruit her as a prostitute, he may *rap* to a *chick* 'make an aggressive verbal approach to a young woman'. *Rapping* refers to any kind of self-confident, aggressive discourse style. The older plantation Black was forced to depend more upon *tomming* (speaking in the manner of Uncle Tom) and *jeffing* (playing up to the white man's expectations—a wild guess about the etymology has put it as a reference to President Thomas Jefferson or to Confederate leader Jefferson Davis).

In plantation society, the field hand spent most of his time in arduous work under the supervision of the overseer. Malingering was severely punished. After work, his contact with whites might be limited to the "pateroller" (patrol officer), who would run him in if he were off his own plantation without a pass. With either of these white men, the Black frequently adopted the verbal strategy of *copping a plea* 'admitting guilt so humbly and persistently as to embarrass the accuser'. British visitor J. F. D. Smyth, whose slave Richmond had failed in his task of minding the master's fishing pole, heard this example in 1784:

now, massa, me know me deserve good flogging, cause if great fish did jump into de canoe, he see me asleep, den he jump out again, and I no catch him; so, massa, me willing now take good flogging.[35]

As might be expected, Smyth did not flog or even punish his slave.

Another verbal strategy important to surviving slavery and degraded social status was *loud talking*, getting at an otherwise invulnerable offender by speaking up about his offense in an embarrassing context. (To be really effective, the loud talker should also employ *signifying*, indirect statement or suggestion.) With what sociologist John Dollard in *The Shadow of the Plantation* called "the sexual advantage," Southern owners would undoubtedly have spawned a much greater number of mixed-blood children if slave women had not known the strategy of subtly calling attention to hereditary resemblances in the presence of the owner's wife.

With the end of slavery and a partial shift in the American caste structure, the disguise function and the coping function of Black verbal performance became less essential than they once were. A positive value is still attached, however, to verbal strategies; to "belong" in the Black community is partly a matter of using the slang. Among adolescent male groups like Manhattan's Morningside Heights Thunderbird gang, a hierarchy of verbal skills is to be observed.[36] On the fringes, *lames* engage in futile attempts to *run with the gang*, 'use the slang', and play the dozens, but can't quite keep up. *Squares* don't know there's any running going on, and *sissies* would be appalled at the activities or the language of the group.

The hierarchy of verbal skills is clear-cut. There is, however, another hierarchy in another kind of verbal skill. In reading, the order of proficiency is exactly reversed, with the sissies at the top and the leaders of the gang at the bottom.[37] In a nation in which literacy is virtually requisite to employment, ghetto language ability correlates highly with joblessness and negatively with success.

More advantaged middle-class Americans, almost all of them white, have been attracted to the language of the ghetto and to some of the more superficial of its values. These whites have become known by the name *hippies*, originally a derogatory term for a would-be *hipster* who couldn't quite make it. (Dalby has shown that *hip* is an Africanism, citing Wolof *hipi* 'to open one's eyes, to be aware of what is going on'.) Much of the hippies' slang comes from the Blacks. The hippie defines himself as the opposite of the *redneck*, who has fewer resemblances to Black culture. Since the hippie got into Black-influenced music after the bop revolution of the 1950's led by Charlie

Parker, Dizzy Gillespie, and Charlie Christian, he uses *cool* as the term of universal approbation. Smoking marijuana, commonplace among jazz musicians even in the days before it was illegal, is another strong distinguishing characteristic of the hippie; to be *cool* is likely to mean, for him, 'to be favorable toward the use of marijuana'. "Smoking" is not, however, an indispensable feature; anyone who promotes the hippie life style without attracting "hassles" from authority figures like the police, school officials, or parents may be "cool." There is a feeling among some hippies that to smoke marijuana ostentatiously, not as a matter of *doin' your own thing*, is uncool.

But the aesthetic principles of the cool movement that culminated in Miles Davis are completely foreign to the hippies. Their music comes from another part of the Black tradition, rock and roll. It is loud—almost always amplified electronically—and frenetic, but the term *hot* is not used to refer to it. For the hippie, *rock* is an etymologically unexamined musical term. There is little doubt, however, that it reflects a sexual metaphor: "My baby rocks me with one steady roll." *Roll*, the silent partner in the combination insofar as hippies are concerned, is an active one for the Blacks:

> Say, you must be wantin' me, baby, to break
>   my back — No!
> Sweet mama rollin' . . .
> Sweet mama rollin' stone.
>
> Tell me, mama, how you want your rollin' done.
> Sweet mama rollin' . . .
> Sweet mama rollin' stone.[38]

Hippies use rock music as, among other things, background music for drug consumption, producing a condition labeled *stoned* 'totally involved', taken over from the originally Black intensifier in phrases like *stone blind* and *my stone friend*. For Blacks, on the other hand, the music serves for dancing. Historically, names like Camel Walk, Buzzard Lope, Fish Tail, Snake Hip, Giouba, Dog Scratch and others have revealed African associations.[39] In the Jazz Age of the twenties, the related Black dance, the Charleston, revolutionized American white ballroom dancing, and further developments like *jitterbugging* have put their stamp on almost all popular entertainment.

However, the apparent recent increase in Black influence is partly illusory. The drug culture, at least as great an influence as the Black, is responsible for song titles like "Yellow Submarine" (downers) and "Eat a Peach" (hallucinogenic mushroom). The jazz scene of the twenties had *viper* 'a marijuana user', which the hippies have not picked up, and *roach* 'a marijuana cigarette', which they have—with the semantic change that it is now the unsmoked remnant of a "joint." The simple report studies of hippie language that have been made so far permit no real conclusions as to the degree of influence, but it seems a safe guess that about fifty percent of it is Black. Hippies continue to address each other as *man*, for example, but few have changed to *dude* with the Black fashion.

Much of the "hip" slang is not so strikingly new as is often believed. A great deal of it is paralleled in the speech patterns of plantation Blacks in the nineteenth century, although in most cases some semantic change has taken place. There is, for example, the participle *busted*, long familiar in white slang in the sense 'broke, without funds' which was replaced in the sixties by the meaning 'arrested'. A person who had been busted was likely to be *on ice* 'in prison'. Although the hippies and their associates might use *busted* for even such minor infractions as traffic violations, the most characteristic use of the term was for being picked up by the vice squad for prostitution or drug use. Harrison's "Negro English" of the 1880 records the expression *to get busted* 'to fail', which could lead by easy semantic transference (the subject failed to evade the fuzz) to the present meaning.

The contemporary use of *heavy* to mean 'arcane, profound' also has its plantation progenitors. In the inner city today, *heavy knowledge* (also *heavy stuff* or *heavy shit*) generally refers to a kind of occultism associated with the Black Muslims, their concept of Allah, and their racio-political line of reasoning. As collected by Labov, Cohen, Robins, and Lewis, it is highly eschatological in nature:

> Dig that—the *laast* days of that *ye-ear* when all people— we'll have succeeded in becomin' a dominant people under Christ Revelation, when all people will come to know our knowledge, wisdom, 'n' understanding that we are the sons of men.[40]

In spite of the demonstrated fact that *heavy* knowledge was the latest thing in Harlem hipness in the 1960's, neither the term nor the attitude should have been a surprise to anyone halfway conversant with Afro-American anthropology. In *Suriname Folk-Lore* (1936), Herskovits and Herskovits reported the use of the same term in a strikingly similar sense among the Blacks of Paramaribo, Surinam:

> Thus comment is made that *Kromanti* dancing is *hebi*— "difficult"—that is "strong," or "dangerous." . . . The *Kromanti winti* are conceived as powerful spirits, who when they possess human beings, cause them to speak African words not intelligible to the uninitiated.[41]

Gullah folk-tale collector Ambrose Gonzales lists *hebby* 'great' in the Glossary to his *Black Border* and cites *uh hebby complain'* 'a great outcry'.

Hippies and other derivative and imitative groups are not always aware of the Afro-American cultural patterns in which Black slang is rooted. Nor do they have access to the out-of-awareness sense of tradition that a ghetto Black can draw upon. They have "picked up on" the in-group identification feature of Black slang but have not mastered either the cultural background or the productive devices. A few inversions exist among the motorcycle gangs, as the world learned when Hell's Angels made the headlines and it was discovered that the girl friend of a member was his "ol' lady." Beyond that, there is little that expresses the spirit rather than the letter of Black verbal performance. Whites play the dozens, especially in the South, but their insults tend to be ritualized and stereotyped rather than creative as among Blacks. In this respect, the adult white player of the dozens reaches about the level of a preteen beginner in the ghetto, who memorizes a few responses (if someone says to him, "You favver ain't no man," he is able to respond, "You muvver like it") as an initial stage of learning to "play."

Playing the dozens had a real value for the Blacks in that it provided a way of retaining self-respect even under humiliating conditions like slavery. The origin of the term is lost to history; perhaps the best guess is that *putting* [a slave] *in the dozens* meant classifying one with that part of the human merchandise which had been damaged in the middle passage so that he could not even be sold as an individual but had to be offered with eleven others. But the earliest recorded example shows how an African on a slave ship managed a verbal comeback to a white slaver whom he would not have dared to challenge on any other terms. Told that a recently captured monkey of large size and unusual color could be his wife, the African replied, "No, this no my Wife, this a white Woman, this fit Wife for you."[42] William Smith, the captain of the slave ship, considered that "this unlucky Wit of the Negroe's . . . hastened the Death of the Beast, for the next Morning it was found dead under the Windless."

Until commercial exploitation made jazz and some of its

vocabulary known in the 1920's, Black language forms had been very little known. Because their musical terms and their expressions for private and personal interaction were unfamiliar, Blacks were assumed to use the same vocabulary as Southern whites. In fact, they were considered rather more Southern than the whites of Alabama or Louisiana, since the whites traveled a great deal and the Blacks did not. As a nonmobile part of the population, Blacks were supposed to speak the nearest thing we had to a truly regional dialect. Those who sampled their language concentrated on farm terms (*string beans* or *snap beans; slop bucket, swill pail* or *swill bucket; hay stack, hay barrack,* or *hay doodle; corn husk* or *corn shuck; wish bone* or *pulley bone; corn bread, corn pone,* or *johnny cake*). They found, predictably, little or no difference from Southern whites, since the whites owned the farms and the agricultural implements that the sharecropping blacks had to use and were able to control the terminology. With the expansion of linguistic research into other domains, motivated by the sometimes harsh criticism of the new sociolinguists, much greater differences are being discovered. It has been found, for example, that in a given area only certain Black speakers will say *Higo* (*Here go*), 'here is' or 'here are', and Dago (*there go*), 'there is' or 'there are'. Whereas a middle-class child, describing the falling of a rock into the water, will say that it "*goes* splash!" the speaker of Black English Vernacular will report that it "*say* splash!" Black speakers use zero copula (*he sick* for *he is sick*) and the unmarked possessive (*he book* for *his book*) more than even white children who have been in extensive contact with Blacks. And the Black vernacular has phrases like *You been know dat!* 'You've known that a long time' that most white speakers don't even understand.[43]

The attitudinal change that made the Black vocabulary from something almost unknown into a part of almost general American English usage was the result of an important sociological phenomenon, the revolt of middle-class youth in the 1960's.[44] Thus, although Blacks were present in great numbers before 1665, their greatest influence on the American vocabulary took place around 1960. As everyone knows, a great part of that impact has reached England.[45] Indeed, some of it has come back to America from Great Britain through the medium of British rock groups like the Beatles and the Rolling Stones. The full scope of the Black influence, and what has happened to the Black terms in their migration first to the Northern cities and then to the entire world, would make another book in itself.

8

Advertisers, Politicians, and Other Hucksters

Since at least as early as the beginning of the nineteenth century, Americanization of English has been associated in many people's minds with the debasement of the language, and American advertising has been cited as one of the major debasers. Advertising jargon is no recent development. Even before the end of the eighteenth century, if we can trust the records, American housewives were being tempted to extravagance by advertisements in newspapers—and husbands were being driven to despair by their wives' expenditures. In "Account of a Buyer of Bargains" (1797) a husband reports

> I had often observed that advertisements set her [his wife] on fire, and therefore . . . I forbade the newspaper to be taken any longer.[1]

In 1803, an "English gentleman lately returned from America" reported his "Animadversions on the Present State of Literature and Taste in the United States":

> One third of the American newspaper is filled with uncouth advertisements written, in general, in language, and abounding in phrases, wholly unintelligible to the English reader.[2]

The phrase "unintelligible to the English reader" is probably one of the exaggerations typical of such statements; but obviously something was happening to the language of the United States, and it was expressed as directly in advertising as in anything else.

Many other observers reported the prominence of advertising in the public functions of American English, that being one of the domains in which it gained an early advantage over competing languages. Benjamin Franklin, for example, complained about the persistence of German in Pennsylvania. German speakers imported books from their homeland, and of the six publishing houses in Pennsylvania, two published exclusively in German, one published half in German and half in English, and two (from Franklin's point of view, "only" two) published exclusively in English. Street signs had inscriptions in both languages, and in some places only in German. But advertisements, "intended to be general," were printed in English as well as in German.[3]

To disseminate the advertisements, early Americans had nothing like the electronic media (radio, movies, television). There were, nevertheless, methods other than newspapers and magazines. One of the most successful was the traveling medicine show, with a certain amount of entertainment thrown in so that a crowd would gather to listen to the pitch. Some of the shows involved the services of minstrels, both black and white. Where the commercial-theatre minstrel show used white performers in blackface, the medicine show was multiethnic and multicolored. It included an Indian component from very early times.

The Indian medicine show peddled "Indian" herb medicines along with free entertainment. Indians would arrive in a New England town and boil medicinal herbs in front of their tents. One of the earliest groups was the Kickapoo Indian Medicine Company—surely an inspiration, at some remove, for the Kickapoo Joy Juice of *Li'l Abner*'s Lonesome Polecat and Hairless Joe.

The Indian medicine show apparently began as a white enterprise. Some clever fellow was able to exploit the popular belief in Indian "medicine"—and, of course, the popular half-understanding of that concept. (See Chapter 6.) One John E. Healey, who named himself variously "Doc." or "Col.", conceived the idea of having real Indians give the pitch for "Indian Herb Medicine." Such employment—or exploitation—of Indians in the medicine shows was a forerunner of sentimental Indianism in many phases of advertising, from the use of statues of Indians in front of cigar stores to brand names that suggest the American aborigine.

The term *medicine show,* rather surprisingly, does not appear in the historical dictionaries before the citation from Herbert Asbury's *Sucker's Progress* of 1938. Given Asbury's skill in re-creating an epoch of the past, it seems impossible that he invented the term rather than using an authentic phrase from the period. We know that the show itself existed much earlier. It utilized Indian *medicine men* (1806), who did a *medicine dance* (1805), by which they evoked the "Great Spirit." They sang *medicine songs* (1791), smoked *medicine pipes* (1833), carried *medicine bags* (1805), talked *medicine talk* (1791), and even lived in *medicine lodges* (1814).[4] The Indians who conducted these curative ceremonies were *powwows* (1624) or *powwow doctors,* the latter phrase sometimes becoming *power doctors* by folk etymology. If the shows in which they participated were not called *medicine shows,* even though the term is not attested for that date by the historical dictionaries, something is strangely amiss.

The importance of medicine in early American advertising can be explained in part by the scarcity of physicians on the frontier. Many people tried to cure their own illnesses or resorted to whatever remedies might be offered. There was a remarkable growth of medical quackery in the second half of the nineteenth century, producing medicines like "J. L. Curtis's Original Mamaluke Liniment, A sovereign remedy for man and beast" in the Dakota Territory in 1859, and Dr. Williams's Pink Pills for Pale People in the South immediately after the Civil War. Other patent medicines were produced by or attributed to a virtuosic but otherwise unknown Dr. Robertson: Celebrated Stomachic Elixir of Health, Vegetable Nervous Cordial (or Nature's Grand Restorative), Celebrated Gout and Rheumatic Drugs, and Worm Destroying Lozenges. Dr. Godbold's Vegetable Balsam of Life was apparently the work of another great medical mind. The expansion of American newspapers, providing a good medium for promoting the sale of popular remedies like these, contributed to the expanding market for patent medicines.[5]

The herb-medicine tradition was commercially important over a long stretch of time. Louis Hebert, reputedly the first Canadian apothecary, was painted consulting with an Indian over herb remedies in 1605. In view of all the modern concern about tobacco as injurious to health, it is startling to find that early America counted the plant among Indian herb medicines. In fact, in the seventeenth century, Europeans considered it a kind of miracle drug from the New World.[6] Some propaganda from the opposition, which in the very early days conceived of tobacco as "stunting a child's growth," seems to have eliminated that idea from popular favor, but in the eighteenth century the concept still cropped up now and then. Even into the nineteenth century the Clingman Tobacco Cure Company of Durham, North Carolina, advertised tobacco cakes and ointment as a cure for bunions, snake bite, scarlet fever, lockjaw, and most other ailments. In the twentieth century, the belief persisted in rural areas that blowing smoke into the aching ear would cure earache.

The debate over smoking and health has always, it seems, been with us, and ad men have always been around to confuse the issue. In the 1940's Old Gold cigarettes advertised "Not a cough in a carload," thus undoubtedly reflecting the apprehension some people felt about the use of "the weed." (*Cigarette cough,* although not represented in the dictionaries, was certainly around by the 1930's.) The Old Gold advertising campaign must have been effective; Lucky Strike found it necessary to adopt a countering tactic: "A treat instead of a treatment."

The cigarette industry's first response to the health question was the adoption of a filter. The term *filter* began to appear in cigarette advertising in the 1940's, and for most Americans unless there is another specific context given, "Does it have a filter?" is automatically assumed to refer to a cigarette. A grimly resigned addicted public adopted *coffin nail* (1901) to describe the cigarette, *cigarette fiend* (1890) to describe the smoker, and *nicotine fit* (not recorded in the historical dictionaries) to describe the withdrawal symptoms of a smoker trying to quit.

Tobacco consumption has been the subject matter of perhaps the biggest, best-planned, and most expensive advertising campaigns in American history. When in 1952 a columnist wanted to compare the "selling" of the Eisenhower-Nixon team to an especially effective advertising campaign, she referred to "patently rehearsed ceremonials borrowed from the tobacco ads."[7]

After tobacco and medicine, politics is probably the biggest customer of American advertising. Vance Packard put it rather strongly:

> By 1952 the Presidency is just another product to peddle through tried-and-true merchandising strategies.[8]

Only occasional politicians like Adlai Stevenson (one of the losers) kept objecting that "the idea that you can mechanize candidates for high office like breakfast cereal . . . is the ultimate indignity to the democratic process."

Actually the "merchandizing" is no new phenomenon. "Tippecanoe and Tyler, Too," the 1840 campaign slogan of General William Henry Harrison, is squarely in that tradition. Harrison's opponent in that race, New Yorker Martin Van Buren, called "Old Kinderhook" because of his birthplace, used the chance similarity of his nickname's initials to the newly popular colloquialism *O.K.* in a clever but eventually ineffective attempt to profit by some sloganism of his own. The term was an Africanism, as David Dalby has shown, picked up from the slaves,[9] but the aggressiveness of Van Buren's campaigns caused even some etymologists to think that his adherents had invented and popularized the expression. The appeal of frontier sloganism was never more perfectly exploited than in Harrison's campaign, which became known to history as the *hard cider campaign.* His adherents were *hard cider* democrats or *hard ciderites* (both from 1840); his program *hard ciderism* (1841); and his congress the *hard cider congress.*

It turned out, however, that the log cabin, which also came into use during the 1840 campaign, was a more potent political symbol than hard cider. The term *log cabin* was originally used to describe a type of housing that seems to have been first used, perhaps by Swedish immigrants, around 1750. Thanks to politicians it came to symbolize solid American frontier virtues. The fact that Abraham Lincoln was born in a log cabin added to his appeal; his administration interrupted a long succession of generals and wealthy landowners in the Presidency. In the comic strip *Li'l Abner,* the wealthy prospective candidate who was reared in the world's largest log cabin by his politically ambitious parents captures the spirit—and some of the absurdity—of this part of our folklore.

Ever since 1840, a slogan has been essential to a presidential campaign. Although the statement has been contested,[10] there seems to be no real doubt that "Fifty-four forty or fight" contributed a great deal to the 1844 campaign of James Polk. The slogan promised, of course, to extend the Oregon Territory far into what is now Canada or to wage war. Polk did neither. Americans are, however, accustomed to the failure of both political and advertising slogans. Both Woodrow Wilson and Franklin D. Roosevelt won second terms as Presidents who "kept us out of war," and war was declared during the second term of each. For that matter, not every little boy who eats his Wheaties becomes a champion athlete. In both domains, politics and advertising, slogans have become a kind of phatic communication. The catchiness of the slogan is the important thing, not the semantic content of the words.

Both Abraham Lincoln and Franklin Roosevelt, facing reelection in wartime, made capital of the rural proverb "Don't change horses in midstream" as a campaign slogan. Horses were an important factor in American life when Lincoln ran, but not when Roosevelt used them. His slogan was part of the rather self-conscious appeal to frontier life that has remained a large part of the vocabulary of politics. Rather than stressing the supermodern, as other public-relations efforts usually do, politics depends largely on allusion to the American past. It uses the homey vocabulary of the backwoods in such phrases as *pump priming, slice of the melon,* and *log-rolling.* "Distribution of governmental largesse to political adherents" is a pale description alongside *pork barrel.*

The last expression, meaning 'a barrel in which pork is kept', was used as early as 1801, but even that citation refers proverbially to "minding our pork and cider barrels"—thus symbolically to property in general. The figurative meaning 'funds for local improvements designed to ingratiate congressmen with their constituents' is not attested before 1913, but it must have existed earlier since *pork barrel bill* is recorded for the same year. Contacting his most important constituents is *getting back to the grassroots* for the American politician, even one whose voters are predominantly urban. The *full dinner pail* is one of the few expressions appealing to both urban and rural workers equally.

Both rural and urban voters expect the politicians to *talk turkey*. The phrase is attested, although with little explanation, from 1835. *The Life and Adventures* of Black Indian trader James P. Beckwourth (published in 1856 but reporting events of twenty years or so before) quotes a Pawnee Loup Indian whom a white man was trying to swindle in a proposed treaty as saying that the document "talked all turkey" to the white man and "all crow" to the Indian tribe. *Talk turkey* in that sense means something like 'tell me what's in it for me that is really worth having'.

If he fails to get reelected, a congressman is in for a session as a *lame duck*. This term has been in use in British English since 1761, in the sense of 'a disabled person or thing', specifically in Stock Exchange slang for 'one who cannot meet his financial obligations; a defaulter'. In the sense of 'an office-holder who has not been reelected', it is purely American, first attested in 1863. It is especially applicable to a congressman who has lost the election and is participating in a short legislative session. *Dead duck,* perhaps an analogical development from the other *duck* term, was originally political. It was used from 1867 on in the sense of 'one who is without influence politically, bankrupt, or played out'. More recent usage applies it to a defeated or hopeless person—more or less like the Western *gone coon* or the rural *gone goose.* Ranching terminology is not especially important in the American congress, except for *maverick*. A *dark horse candidate* probably refers to horse-racing rather than to ranching.

In keeping with the old-fashioned emphases of political terminology, Indians have retained an important place in the vocabulary. Tammany Hall, for example, was named for a Delaware Indian chief, although most Americans I have questioned about it thought it referred to an Irishman. The original Tammany was famous for his love of liberty and for his wisdom. William Mooney, who founded the Tammany organization and named it after the Delaware Tamanend, introduced the affectation of using Indian titles in 1789. The thirteen trustees of the organization, called *sachems,* symbolized the thirteen original states; the president of the organization was the *grand sachem;* and the President of the United States, up to the time of Andrew Jackson, was the *great grand sachem.* In the 1920's Al Smith was known as "the Tammany brave."

Words like *caucus,* from the Algonquian, still play an important part in national legislative action. Others, like *mugwump,* are further from their original Indian meaning. *Mugwump* is perhaps the extreme case, having gone from meaning 'a very important person' to signifying 'a fence sitter' (mug on one side, wump on the other). But losing the original meaning is not unusual in the field of political terminology: Boss Flynn of Chicago inspired the expression "In like Flynn," because he always won; but when movie actor Errol Flynn got into some much-publicized trouble with what we would now call groupies in the mid-forties, the phrase came to mean something quite different. Semantic changes take place easily in the domain of politics, and it matters little what language the terms originally came from.

There are enough Indian terms in politics to make them seem quite normal. It was nothing unusual, for example, when the powerful New Orleans Ring organization, which had kept the city under white supremacy rule throughout almost all of the third quarter of the nineteenth century, regrouped under the name of the Choctaw Club after it was defeated by a reformist group. The familiarity of non-Anglo-Saxon terms in politics probably facilitated the adoption of words of problematic origin like *scalawag* and *snollygoster,* and the free and easy word-forming of the multilingual early American society no doubt expedited the adoption of new compounds like *carpetbaggers.* A compound like *muckraker* seems, in the American context, especially appropriate to 'one who makes charges of corruption on the part of politicians and governmental figures'. *The Oxford English Dictionary* cites one example of *muckrake* 'to rake refuse together' in British English, but the figurative meaning is strictly American. The noun *muckraker,* in the American sense, is attested as early as 1871 and enjoyed a real vogue in the early twentieth century applied to writers like Lincoln Steffens. *Muckraking,* in the phrase *muckraking reformers,* is first reported in 1906.

Except for a certain amount of scientific terminology in the claims made by popular drugs (now greatly restricted by federal law), advertising, like politics, has preferred to recombine everyday vocabulary elements into new compounds rather than to use Latin- and Greek-derived elements as scientists do. Our soaps, medicines, cigarettes, and politicians have sold better when they were advertised in a homey, slightly old-fashioned vocabulary. Most of our really big promotional schemes, whether in business or in politics, have been rural- and frontier-oriented.

Why should this be so, when our society prides itself on being mechanized and technological? Why do we go to the drive-in window at the bank in an automobile whose name commemorates the premechanical days of the frontier? Automobiles with names of more effete reference, like Grand Prix, El Dorado, Riviera, Monaco, and Malibu are not unknown, but the market is dominated by Bronco, Pinto, Charger, Colt, Mustang, Maverick, Cougar, Wildcat, Bobcat, Hawk, Falcon, Skylark, and Rabbit (with which Volkswagen gets into the American spirit of things). Hornet, the old Hudson, is so much in the spirit of things that American Motors has recently revived the name. The Indian past is also evoked, largely for its exoticism, in automobile names. Pontiac, the name of an Indian chief, has long been with us, and Chevrolet has recently come up with a Cheyenne model. But the most blatant commercial use of Indian lore has been Ford's Thunderbird. This creature with an extra head on its abdomen was especially important to the Haida of the Northwest Coast, whose carvings of it are still extant. Conspicuous consumption in automobiles (the lean little T-bird of the 1950's was designed as a second car for people who found their Cadillacs too cumbersome to park downtown, although its contemporary namesake is decidely overstuffed) is bizarrely consistent with a pretense of arcane knowledge about Indian tribal customs.

Why does so much history survive in the terminology of an assembly-line product whose prophet, Henry Ford, proclaimed, "History is bunk?" Why do we have football teams named Longhorns, Mustangs, Lions, Cowboys, Plainsmen, Badgers, Bruins, Golden Bears, etc., in the "athletic" entertainment carefully tailored for our television screens, and only one with a "business" name like the Packers? (The New York Mets, Jets, and Nets are perhaps symptomatic of another trend developing, but they haven't been around long enough for the onomastic pattern to become clear. Whether the name had anything to do with it or not, the Shreveport Steamers didn't last even one entire season.) It would be easy to explain this phenomenon in terms of "the American spirit" or "the enduring ideals of the frontier," but the answer is prob-

ably more mundane—culture lag. The frontier itself was
the biggest promotional scheme in our history. We have
carried over the habits of the past rather than consciously
innovating.

Those who moved westward did not do so simply because they spontaneously felt the urge. It may not have
been only Horace Greeley's "Go West, Young Man" that
did the trick, but his and other slogans probably had as
much to do with it as the desire for adventure. The real
advance guard, like the mountain men, was motivated
both by the desire for what gain could be realized from
the sale of furs and by the easy availability of Indian
women, a welcome contrast to the frigidity of the Puritan
girls back home.[11] It is no accident that a promise of sex
(the girl in the bikini may go with the car or the Coca-
Cola) is a major part of the best advertising techniques.
But for the larger groups who ventured out toward the
Oregon Territory and other areas, it took a promotional
scheme of fantastic proportions to instil any urge to move
away from the comforts of the East.

With the movement for territorial expansion and free
land, the country entered upon one of the greatest advertising campaigns in history—the "booming" of the West.
(The verb *boom,* from a noun originally Dutch, was first
applied to a river, in the meaning 'rush strongly', around
1831; by 1884, *booming* meant 'splendid, grand'; the sense
of 'in a period of great economic activity' came shortly
thereafter.)* This was a campaign in which orators and
politicians participated as much as railroad companies and
land salesmen, departments and bureaus of agriculture
and other farmers' organizations, boards of trade, and
chambers of commerce. Countless speeches were made in
support of it, and promotional activity included inspi-
rational literature in immigrant handbooks, railroad

---

* See Chapter 2 for material on the ultimate derivation of *boom.*

guides, state and regional gazetteers, rural almanacs, real estate directories, and government reports.

The people involved in these activities were *boosters*. This term, in the sense of 'one who supports or promotes given interests', arose in the West in the 1890's and soon spread to general advertising and chamber of commerce activities. The booster was the type Sinclair Lewis satirized so brilliantly in *Babbitt* and *Main Street,* but without dissuading Americans from "boosting"—in fact, Lewis' conscious exaggerations seemed to give them some new ideas. The opposite of the booster was, of course, the *knocker,* who dared to see that every money-making or expansion scheme wasn't perfect. Even the churches were against knocking. In the 1930's, Southern Baptist Sunday school children sang, to the tune of "Everybody Ought to Love Jesus," "Everybody Ought to Be a Booster":

> Everybody ought to be a booster, a booster, a booster.
> A booster never knocks, and a knocker never boosts.
> Everybody ought to be a booster.

Lincoln Steffens had one of his cartoonists do a picture of a burglar, caught in the act and menaced by a policeman's club, saying "Don't knock; boost."

Americans have continued to revel in the kind of ballyhoo by which the West was won. Historically, there can be little doubt of the importance of this promotional rhetoric. B. A. Botkin has put it exceptionally well.

> Besides manifest destiny, free land, and state pride, the West had another string to its bow—the long bow which it drew in order to live down its wild and woolly reputation and to attract settlers. It was the myth of a land flowing with milk and honey—part of the American dream of a promised land of plenty, opportunity, and "beginning," which had first attracted settlers from the

Old World to the New and was now transferred to the
fabulous, far-off West. To make its assets outweigh its
endurances, orators, promotors, and guidebooks painted
this unknown country in the rosy hues of fairyland.[12]

The promotional terminology, in its very hyperbole,
was directly comparable to advertising today. The West
was called *the land of Nature's bounty,* or *God's country.*
Perhaps the most characteristic slogan to draw expansion-
minded settlers to the West was "The sky's the limit."
Individual states had their own slogans. Oklahoma was
the Boomer State, or Boomer's Paradise. Illinois and
Kansas each called itself the Garden of the West; New
Mexico was either the Land of Heart's Desire or the Land
of Sunshine. An act of the legislature changed Arkansas
from the Bear State to the Wonder State. California proclaimed that it was the state of perpetual sunshine—and
radio comedians of the 1930's and 1940's told a million
jokes about their homes being washed away by "liquid
sunshine."
Early and late, it was the advertising man who sold the
frontier. The Wyatt Earps and Bat Mastersons really had
nothing to do except be more superlative than anyone
else at slinging a gun—or at holding the pose reasonably
well until a publicity man came around to tell the world
about them. By now dozens of debunking biographies
have been written about these sometimes bogus frontier
heroes, but the country has not wanted to forget the
legendary—as opposed to the historical—frontiersman.
Products bearing the name of Davy Crockett became a
commercial success about one hundred years after his
books had been best sellers.
It is, therefore, not in the least surprising that advertising and ballyhoo continue to stress the frontier spirit,
cattle country, and the rural. A skeptic may wonder just

what a cigarette has to do with all those Western men on horses, but the ads apparently sell cigarettes. Probably not even prizes given for so many box tops have sold as much breakfast cereal as the commercials accompanying serialized Wild West stories on radio and television.

Soap is one of the few commodities that can vie with politics, whiskey, automobiles, and tobacco in competing for the advertiser's minute and dollar. Soap seems an exception to the stress on rural and frontier associations; soap commercials emphasize the mild, new formulas, so different from the lye soap great-grandmother used to make. The ubiquitous soap or detergent advertisement on daytime television (and, earlier, on the radio) justifies the term *soap opera* for the teary dramas that act as come-ons for the soap salesman's pitch. Even that term, however, has a Wild West predecessor: *horse opera,* used of Western and cowboy-type entertainments in general and attested as early as 1857; *soap opera* does not appear until eighty-two years later.

Crass and vulgar as it may be, the triumph of sloganism in American popular communication is overwhelmingly convincing. If you don't believe it, try this simple experiment: Ask fifteen or twenty people, in an interview situation, to quote either a singing commercial for Coca-Cola or two lines from any work by Walt Whitman. Unless you bias the interview by speaking only to Whitman specialists, even university professors will be much more familiar with the soft-drink commercial.

Brand names have played a part in the coinage of new words in American English. Everyone knows how the Kodak Company and Frigidaire suffered because their brand names became common terms for cameras and refrigerators, or how a leading soft-drink manufacturer tried to resist the use of *coke* as a common noun. In everyday usage, *levis* refer to denim trousers without any necessary connection to the trade name from which the term originated. *Simonize* 'to clean and wax the enameled surface of an automobile' has virtually parted company with Simoniz, the trademark from which it originated. In the later nineteenth century, Merry Widow was a brand name for rubber prophylactic devices. By around 1930, *merry widow* designated such a contraceptive, and a reference to Lehar's operetta would bring snickers in rural America. The term became obsolete in the 1940's, possibly because the product couldn't compete with Trojans. The name of the University of Southern California football team inspired its share of leers during the forties and fifties, and the familiarity of the brand name made Homer's *Iliad* an obscene text to some.

The richness of compounds (noun modifying noun, as in *sherry cobbler* and *baby sitter*), which the earliest observers found in American English, is today nowhere more in evidence than in the common nouns borrowed from advertising. Many phrases that originated there are now part of our basic vocabulary: *do-it-yourself, back-to-school (sale), wash-and-wear* (or *drip-dry*), *ready-mix (cement* or *cake), all-purpose (gloves* or *soap), handy-wipe, off-the-rack.* The phrase *ready-to-wear* has developed since the 1930's, superseding phrases like *ready for wearing.*[13]

The commercialism of American life is openly and frankly manifested, as it has been in almost no other culture of the past or present. There is obvious hypocrisy in our sentimental attitude toward the Indian in our advertising, but probably no more than in the Renaissance English sentimentality toward the Arthurian legends, dealing with a Celtic people long ago conquered and subjected to exploitation. The positive thinking that our advertisers and commercial people took over from the boosters of our frontier past dominates every aspect of our life. When the American merchandizer doesn't want to fool with returned bottles for soft drinks, he labels them *Disposable* or *No*

Return. When the ecology movement forces him to change that policy, he continues to accentuate the positive by calling them *Money-Back Bottles*. Nothing else would be possible in our society. It's the American way.

Notes

Chapter 1

[1] Sabir was virtually ignored for a very long time, although there have been a number of articles recently. Hugo Schuchardt, "Die Lingua Franca," *Zeitschrift für Romanische Philologie,* 1909, is the classical source. An even more specialized work is Kahane, Kahane, and Tietze, *The Lingua Franca in the Levant: Turkish Nautical Terms of Italian and Greek Origin,* Urbana, Illinois, 1958. The most important article linking Sabir to the New World pidgins and creoles is probably Keith Whinnom's "The Origin of the European-based Pidgins and Creoles," *Orbis,* 1965.

[2] In addition to the works listed in footnote 1, there are tantalizing hints in books like J. C. Hotten's *The Slang Dictionary* (1887, reprinted 1972): "The vulgar dialect of Malta and the Scala towns of the Levant—imported into this country and incorporated with English cant—is known as the Lingua Franca, or bastard Italian" (p. 2). Schuchardt also makes the point that the earliest form of Lingua Franca was predominantly Italian in vocabulary, probably because of the early prominence of the Italian city-states in Mediterranean shipping. The possible relationship of Lingua Franca to English "slang" or "cant" has been developed in an article by Ian F. Hancock (see Bibliography).

[3] *Hakluytus Posthumus, or Purchas His Pilgrimes,* Vol.

18:277 ("The Voyage of Monsieur de Montis into New France, written by Marke Lescarbot," A.D. 1606).

⁴ Robert A. Hall, Jr., *Pidgin and Creole Languages,* Cornell University Press, 1966, p. 100.

⁵ See Hall, *Haitian Creole,* 1953; and Jules Faine, *Le Creole dans l'Univers,* 1939. Both of these take the notion of the actual linguistic content as representing "Norman" French more seriously than I am inclined to do.

⁶ See Michael Silverstein, "Dynamics of Recent Linguistic Contact," in I. Goddard (ed.), *Handbook of North American Indian Languages,* Vol. XVI (forthcoming). A summary of some of Silverstein's main points will appear in Emanuel J. Drechsel, "An Essay on Pidginization and Creolization of North American Indian Languages, with a Note on Indian English, *International Journal of the Sociology of Language,* 1976.

⁷ See Whinnom, *op. cit.,* and Paul Christophersen's two articles in *English Studies,* 1953 and 1959.

⁸ The extremely diverse nature of American Indian languages can be appreciated after an examination of a work like Franz Boas, *Handbook of American Indian Languages,* 1911, 2 vols.

⁹ J. Dyneley Prince, "An Ancient New Jersey Indian Jargon," *American Anthropologist* 14:508.

¹⁰ *Ibid.*

¹¹ Lorenzo Johnston Greene, *The Negro in Colonial New England, 1620–1776,* Columbia University Studies in History, Economics, and Public Law, No. 494, p. 198.

¹² William Fitzwilliam Owen, *Voyages to Explore the Shores of Africa, Arabia, and Madagascar,* London, 1833, I:29.

¹³ See *Black English,* Random House, 1972, Chapter III.

¹⁴ Justin Winsor (ed.), *The Memorial History of Boston, Including Suffolk County, Massachusetts, 1630–1880,* Boston, 1882, p. 477.

¹⁵ "A Merchant of Boston," *The Present State of Eng-*

land, quoted by Kittredge, *The Old Farmer and His Almanac,* 1912, p. 354.

[16] Cf. *me no stomany* 'I don't understand' and *Now me stomany that* 'Now I understand that' in Sarah Kemble Knight's *Journal* (1704).

[17] It is a linguistic commonplace that American Indian languages, like some other non-Indo-European languages, have "whisper" vowels, without the vibration of the vocal chords in the way that we tend to regard as essential to vowels. (For the approximate effect, try pronouncing *a day* or another phrase consisting of *a* plus a monosyllabic noun by whispering the article and pronouncing the noun with full voice.) This is an accepted fact, but apparently no studies of borrowings from American Indian languages have given any special attention to it.

[18] William Safire, review of *All-American English, New York Times Book Review,* May 18, 1975, p. 4, treats this opinion as though it were beyond question. George Philip Krapp, *The American Language* (I:106) counted "all of the words of Indian origin, exclusive of personal, place, and other proper names . . . that have had at some time or another greater or less currency as English words." He came up with more than 230 words. Most recent treatments contain some phrase like "about fifty words of Indian language origin."

[19] *American English,* 1958, p. 32.

[20] Christopher Ward, *The War of the Revolution,* Macmillan, 1952, p. 143.

[21] Quoted in Morris Bishop, "Four Indian Kings in London," *American Heritage,* December 1971, p. 74.

[22] Jack D. Forbes, *The Indian in America's Past,* Prentice-Hall, p. 39.

[23] Peter Wood, *Black Majority,* Knopf, 1974, p. 59.

[24] Forbes, *op. cit.,* p. 99.

[25] Page Smith, *John Adams,* I:5.

[26] Quoted in Forbes, *op. cit.,* p. 199.

[27] Meridel LeSueur, *North Star Country*, New York, 1945, p. 156.

[28] Richardson, *Beyond the Mississippi*, 1867, p. 486.

[29] *The New World Negro* (ed. Frances Herskovits), Indiana University Press, 1966, p. 284.

[30] Hans Nathan, *Dan Emmett and the Rise of Early Negro Minstrelsy*, University of Oklahoma Press, 1962, p. 11.

Chapter 2

[1] Melville J. Herskovits, "Gods and Familiar Spirits," in *The New World Negro* (ed. Frances Herskovits), Indiana University Press, 1966, p. 284.

[2] O. G. T. Sonneck, *Report on the Star-Spangled Banner, Hail Columbia, America, and Yankee Doodle*, Washington, 1909, p. 111.

[3] Geoffrey D. Needler, "Linguistic Evidence from Alexander Hamilton's *Itinerarium*," *American Speech*, October 1967, p. 210.

[4] Smith, *John Adams*, I:54.

[5] Needler, *op. cit.*, p. 215.

[6] For an illuminating account of the contemporary situation, see Jan Voorhoeve, "Varieties of Creole in Suriname," in Dell Hymes (ed.), *Pidginization and Creolization of Languages*, Cambridge University Press, 1971.

[7] *Crumbs from an Old Dutch Closet*, The Hague, 1938, p. 39.

[8] This is approximately the dialect of *Uncle Tom's Cabin*. Since Mrs. Stowe knew New York better than Natchitoches Parish, Louisiana, it is probable that she projected the dialect of her own area into the region about which she had scanty knowledge. For a much better rendition of the Louisiana Black dialect of the nineteenth century, see Kate Chopin, *Bayou Folk*.

[9] Frances D. Gage, transcript quoted in Elizabeth Cady Stanton, Susan B. Anthony, and Matilda Joslyn Gage (eds.), *History of Woman Suffrage,* Rochester, New York, 1889, pp. 165–66.

[10] *Dialect Notes,* 1910, p. 459.

[11] Gertrude Leffert Vanderbilt, *The Social History of Flatbush,* New York, 1881, p. 53.

[12] *Ibid.,* p. 55.

[13] Prince, *op. cit.,* p. 464.

[14] Saxby V. Penfold, *Romantic Suffern,* Tallman, N.Y., 1955.

[15] Edwin Newman, *Strictly Speaking,* Bobbs-Merrill, 1974, p. 157, quotes this as an example of "bad" English, in a context of insistence that American English is undergoing some kind of deterioration. On the same page, Newman refers to Muhammad Ali's *flustrated,* evidently as an example of the same kind of "corruption." Actually, neither form is especially unusual in Black English. A story on a Black convicted murderer in the Houston *Chronicle* for November 14, 1965 (Section 2, p. 2), quoted him as complaining about his "life of flustrations."

[16] See Ian F. Hancock, "A Provisional Comparison of the English-based Atlantic Creoles," *African Language Review* VII (1969):7–72. Since this theory about relexification of Pidgin English with Dutch etymons is controversial even among professional creolists, I have continued to refer in this book to a Pidgin Dutch origin for Dutch Creole.

[17] A representative treatment is that of D. C. Hesseling, *Het Negerhollands der Deense Antillen,* Leiden, 1905. Popular belief that Virgin Islands speakers spoke "Danish" Creole, because the islands were owned by Denmark and because the plantation owner group was largely Danish, greatly overestimates the influence of Europeans on the language of the West Africa–derived population.

[18] Van Loon, *Crumbs from an Old Dutch Closet,* p. 46.

[19] See the statement of Captain Marryat, in a context of commenting on names for cocktails, quoted in Chapter 5.

[20] Matthew St. Clair Clarke, *The Life of David Crockett, the Original Humorist and Irrepressible Backwoodsman, An Autobiography*, New York, n.d.

[21] Samuel P. Orth, *Our Foreigners: A Chronicle of Americans in the Making*, New Haven, 1920, p. 153.

Chapter 3

[1] This particular *y'awl* is probably a calque (a filling in of an African structure with English material) from *unu*, the West African second person plural pronoun also used in Gullah, Jamaican Creole, and the dialects of many other West Indian islands. Jay Edwards ("African Influences on the English of San Andres Island, Colombia," in Hancock and DeCamp [eds.], *Pidgins and Creoles: Current Trends and Prospects*, 1972) points out that in the Creole English of San Andres both *you all* and *unuaal* occur. Edwards asserts: "In the white plantation English of Louisiana, the form *y'all* functioned precisely as did the *unu* of the slaves. The use of *y'all* (semantically *unu*) was probably learned by white children from black mammies and children in familiar domestic situations" (p. 14).

[2] Hans Kurath, *A Phonology and Morphology of Modern English*, Heidelberg, Carl Winter, 1964, p. 120.

[3] See, for example, the diphthongal treatment in George L. Trager and Henry Lee Smith, *Outline of the Structure of English*, 1951.

[4] John Peale Bishop, *Collected Essays*, 1933, p. 99.

[5] Mima Babington and E. Bagby Atwood, "Lexical Usage in Southern Louisiana," *Publications of the American Dialect Society* 36 (November 1961):11.

[6] Herbert Asbury, *The French Quarter*, p. 100.

[7] Charles Gayarré, "The New Orleans Bench and Bar in 1823," *Harper's Magazine,* Vol. 77 (1881).

[8] *Ibid.,* p. 889.

[9] *Ibid.,* p. 888.

[10] *Ibid.,* p. 889.

[11] Cable, *Old Creole Days,* p. 99.

[12] Gayarré, *op. cit.,* p. 894.

[13] Harnett T. Kane, *The Bayous of Louisiana,* William Morrow, 1943, p. 322.

[14] The first two of the quotations are from Chopin's *A Night in Acadie,* 1897, pp. 190 and 203, respectively. The third is from the short story "Loka" in the collection *Bayou Folk,* 1894.

[15] Ramsey, *Cajuns on the Bayous,* 1957, p. 160.

[16] *Ibid.,* p. 51.

[17] *Ibid.,* p. 49.

[18] Sarah Searight, *New Orleans,* Stein and Day, 1973, p. 101.

[19] Kane, *The Bayous of Louisiana,* p. 325.

[20] See, for example, William W. Chenault and Robert Reinders, "Northern Born Community in New Orleans in the 1880's," *Journal of American History* XC (1972).

[21] Kane, *Queen New Orleans,* New York, 1949, p. 134.

[22] *Ibid.,* p. 235.

Chapter 4

[1] Herbert Asbury, *Sucker's Progress.* This book is exceptionally good on gambling terminology—better than *The Dictionary of Americanisms,* which quotes it extensively. The reader will easily determine that I have been frequently guided by Asbury's work. Additional material of great interest is to be found in his *The Barbary Coast.*

[2] Searight, *New Orleans,* p. 29.

[3] Asbury, *Sucker's Progress,* p. 156.

[4] *Ibid.,* p. 117.

[5] Matsell, *Vocabularium, or the Rogue's Lexicon.*

[6] Rollins, *The Cowboy,* 1936, p. 179.

[7] Barton, *Comic Songster,* 1838.

[8] St. Louis *Reveille,* 1845 (2 May I/6).

[9] Asbury, *Sucker's Progress,* p. 80.

[10] *Ibid.,* p. 205.

[11] Rollins, *op. cit.,* p. 79.

[12] "Poker, Pawns, and Power," in Neil Postman, Charles Weingartner, and Terence P. Moran (eds.), *Language in America,* Pegasus, 1936.

Chapter 5

[1] Mrs. Frances Trollope, *Domestic Manners of the Americans,* Vintage, 1949, p. 279.

[2] Library of Congress Record LP 20, recorded by John A. Lomax.

[3] Trollope, *op. cit.,* p. 241.

[4] *Davy Crockett's Almanac of Wild Sports in the West, Life in the Backwoods, and Sketches of Texas,* Nashville, 1837, I:40.

[5] Tyrone Power, Esq., *Impressions of America During the Years 1833, 1834, and 1835,* London, 1836, I:57.

[6] Ian F. Hancock (personal communication) supplied the information on *kaktel* in Krio.

[7] Searight, *New Orleans,* p. 248.

[8] "A Domestic Origin for the English-derived Atlantic Creoles," *Florida FL Reporter,* 1972.

[9] *The Look of the West,* London, 1860.

[10] James H. Cook, *Fifty Years on the Old Frontier,* University of Oklahoma Press, 1954, p. 188.

[11] Ed. Samuel Cole Williams, New York, 1930, p. 6. On the subject of Indians and whiskey, there are many interesting and revealing Pidgin English attestations like this

one from Thomas Simpson Woodward's *Reminiscences of the Creek or Muscogee Indians,* 1851:

> My friend, you French Chief! me Whiskey John . . . heap my friends, giv me whiskey, drink, am good. White man my very good friend me, white man make whiskey, drink him heap, very good, I drink whiskey . . . You me give one bottle full. I drink him good. Tom Anthony you very good man, me you give one bottle full. You no drink, me drink him all, chaw tobacco little bit, give me some you [p. 70].

[12] Horace Greeley, *Overland Journey from New York to San Francisco in the Summer of 1859,* New York, 1860, p. 201.

[13] Philip Ashton Rollins, *The Cowboy,* 1936, p. 189.

[14] Everett N. Dick, "The Long Drive," *Collections of the Kansas State Historical Society,* Vol. XVII:47.

[15] "Nautical Sources of Krio Vocabulary," *International Journal of the Sociology of Language* VII (1976).

[16] John C. Duval, *The Adventures of Big-Foot Wallace,* 1870, p. 294.

[17] Rollins, *The Cowboy,* p. 79.

[18] Pp. 170–71.

[19] Norman W. Schur, *British Self-Taught, with Comments in American,* Macmillan, 1973.

Chapter 6

[1] *Diary in America with Remarks on Its Institutions,* Philadelphia, 1839, II:30.

[2] Winfred Blevins, *Give Your Heart to the Hawks: A Tribute to the Mountain Men,* Nash Publishing, 1973, p. 53.

[3] *Collections of the Massachusetts Historical Society,* Second Series, VIII:231.

[4] I:14.

[5] I, Series I, 504.

[6] Constance L. Skinner, *Adventures of Oregon: A Chronicle of the Fur Trade,* Yale University Press, 1920, p. 102.

[7] Murray Morgan, *Skid Road: An Informal Portrait of Seattle,* New York, Viking, 1960, p. 7.

[8] Ruxton, *Life in the Far West,* 1848, III:99.

[9] A. B. Guthrie, *The Way West,* 1847, p. 95.

[10] Quoted in Everett N. Dick, *Vanguards of the Frontier,* 1940, p. 59.

[11] Marryat, *op. cit.,* p. 38.

[12] Supplement I:595.

[13] Supplement II:347.

[14] Neihardt, *Black Elk Speaks,* p. 5.

[15] *Life in the Far West,* pp. 165–66.

[16] Skinner, *op. cit.,* p. 103.

[17] Bliss Isley, *Blazing the Way West,* London, 1939, p. 100.

[18] *Life in the Far West,* p. 19 (Ruxton's footnote 33).

[19] Blevins, *op. cit.,* p. 52.

[20] *Life in the Far West,* p. 8.

[21] P. 217.

[22] *Owen Wister Out West, His Journals and Letters* (ed. Fanny Kemble Wister), University of Chicago Press, 1958, p. 153.

[23] *Ibid.,* p. 159.

[24] See Philip L. Durham and Everett L. Jones, *The Negro Cowboys,* Dodd, Mead, 1965; and William Loren Katz, *The Black West,* Doubleday, 1971.

[25] Julian Mason, "The Etymology of *Buckaroo,*" *American Speech,* 1960.

[26] Wister, *op. cit.,* p. 155.

[27] Vance Packard, *The Hidden Persuaders,* David McKay, 1957, p. 167.

[28] Ramon F. Adam's *The Cowman Says It Salty,* Uni-

versity of Arizona Press, 1971, contains a very detailed treatment of the quaint and proverbial language of the cowboy. See also his *Western Words* (1941 and 1968). Many of the materials dealt with in the 1971 work are not known outside the cattle trade, and therefore would not be relevant to this treatment.

[29] For the language of miners, see especially Lincoln Barnett, *The Treasury of Our Tongue,* Knopf, 1964, pp. 188–89. The speech of roughnecks in the oil fields is treated by Lalia Phipps Boone, "Patterns of Innovation in the Language of the Oil Field," *American Speech* 24 (1949): 131–37. Walter McCulloch's *Woods Words* is an outstanding source for the language of the lumberjack of the north woods. There appears to be no adequate treatment of the speech of railway workers.

For miners, although Mark Twain and one or two other well-known writers provide valuable primary data, the most useful original source would seem to be James F. Rusling's *Across America; or, the Great West* (New York, 1875), pp. 72–73. Rusling lists and explains *square meal, shebang, outfit, go down to bed rock, panned out, pay-streak* (not in *A Dictionary of Americanisms,* although it has *pay dirt* from 1856), *peter out,* and *you bet!*

[30] John A. Lomax, "Cowboy Lingo," in Wilson M. Hudson and Alan Maxwell (eds.), *The Sunny Slopes of Long Ago,* Publications of the Texas Folklore Society XXXIII, 1966, p. 117.

Chapter 7

[1] Benjamin Franklin, "Information to Those Who Would Remove to America," in *Writings* (ed. Smythe), VII:606.

[2] Dan Burley, "The Technique of Jive," reprinted from

Dan Burley's Original Handbook of Harlem Jive, in Alan Dundes (ed.), *Mother Wit from the Laughing Barrel,* Prentice-Hall, 1973. *Twister to the slammer* is obviously 'key to the door'. *Dig the jive* means 'perceive what is going on'; it combines the Africanism *dig* (Dalby cites Wolof *dega, deg* 'understand') and what Burley considers a development from English *jibe.* Dalby, however, cites Wolof *jev* 'to talk about someone in his absence'. In all fairness, it should be admitted that neither of these is very convincing. Burley translates *straight up and down, three ways sides and flats* as 'for all she was worth' (*i.e.,* the man to whom the girl gave her door key played her for all she was worth).

³ C. R. Ottley, *How to Talk Old Talk in Trinidad,* Port of Spain, 1965. Ottley gives the following translation:

> She took her revenge out of that one by clandestinely [sic!] bestowing her favours on another until her infidelity came to light. He flogged her. She left the house. She has now transferred her affections to Johnny.

Till de mark buss [i.e., burst] is an unusually transparent example of the relationship between an Afro-American dialect and its Pidgin-Creole background. In WesKos Pidgin English, for example, *pass mark* is an absolute intensifier ('extremely', 'excessively'). *Pass* itself is the normal function word of comparison, something like English *than. Till de mark buss* would be '*WAY* past the mark'! (Obviously, Ottley's very free translation does not indicate those relationships.)

⁴ In the Caribbean, this term is used to both male and female interlocutors (as is *hombre* in Puerto Rican Spanish, for rural speakers). Outsiders frequently misunderstand its import. A psychiatrist named Edwin A. Weinstein (*Cultural Aspects of Delusion: A Psychiatric Study of the Virgin Islands,* Free Press, 1962) was misled by this

use of *man* and by the well-known Creole identity of masculine and feminine pronouns into a fantastic over-statement of the relationship between language and social structure. Less sophisticated observers frequently suspect widespread homosexuality.

[5] Lingua Franca versions of Twi, Yoruba, Wolof, and some other prominent coastal West African languages were in use during the early period. According to Turner, *Africanisms in the Gullah Dialect* (1949), some texts of African-language songs were in use on the Sea Islands in the twentieth century. William A. Stewart (personal communication) suspects that Turner strongly overstated the restriction to the Sea Islands.

[6] Miles Mark Fisher, *Negro Slave Songs in the United States*, Citadel, 1953, *passim*.

[7] *Ibid.*, p. 66.

[8] *Ibid.*, p. 89.

[9] *Ibid.*, p. 111.

[10] *Ibid.*, p. 49.

[11] *Ibid.*, p. 38.

[12] The works of Herskovits cited in this chapter and elsewhere make this point forcefully, but perhaps the most convenient source of concentrated information on the subject is Donald C. Simmons, "Possible West African Sources for the American Negro Dozens," *Journal of American Folklore* LXXVI (October–December, 1963).

[13] Dalby, *op. cit.*, p. 177.

[14] Grace Sims Holt, "Stylin' Outa the Black Pulpit," in Kochman (ed.), *Rappin' and Stylin' Out,* University of Illinois Press, 1972, p. 153.

[15] This point, as well as the complicated relationship between Black speech and underworld usage, is well treated in Nathan Kantrowitz, "The Vocabulary of Race Relations in a Prison," *Publications of the American Dialect Society* LI (April 1969):23–34.

[16] Holt, *op. cit.*, p. 157.

[17] Harold Courlander (ed.), *Ethnic Folkways* 417, notes, p. 11. This use of *bread* is also attested by Guy B. Johnson, "Double Meaning in the Popular Negro Blues," in *Mother Wit from the Laughing Barrel*, p. 261.

[18] Johnson, *Ibid.*

[19] Courlander, *Negro Folk Music, U.S.A.*, pp. 129–30.

[20] Johnson, *op. cit.*, p. 261.

[21] This familiar blues motif can be heard in (e.g.) "Cornbread Blues," sung by Texas Alexander on OK 8511 (recorded December 8, 1927).

[22] Dalby, *op. cit.*, pp. 181–82.

[23] Peg Leg Howell, "New Jelly Roll Blues," Columbia 14210 (recorded August 4, 1927).

[24] Quoted in Johnson, *op. cit.*, p. 261.

[25] P. 252.

[26] These traditional lines are here transcribed directly from "Jelly, Jelly," sung by Billy Eckstein with Earl Hines and an orchestra, recorded in Hollywood on December 2, 1940, and rerecorded on Camden CAL-588.

[27] This is a slight variation on the traditional pattern (thus for *hell* can be substituted *Atlanta, New York, Miami, Texas,* or any other place name). As reported by Alan Lomax (*Negro Folk Songs from the Mississippi State Penitentiary,* Tradition Records TLP 1020, Side B, Band 4), it goes:

> Well, hain't been to Georgia, boys, but,
> Well, it's I been told, sugar,
> Well, hain't been to Georgia, Georgia,
> Well, it's Georgia women, baby,
> Got the sweet jelly roll.

[28] Quoted in LeRoi Jones, *Blues People,* William Morrow, 1963, p. 104.

[29] Quoted in Alan Lomax, *Mr. Jelly Roll,* p. 136.

[30] P. 155 (including footnote). On the association of

early jazzmen with pimps and prostitutes, see any standard treatment. Max Jones and John Chilton, *The Louis Armstrong Story*, Little, Brown, 1971, p. 56, give a characteristically restrained account of Louis' early dabbling in that activity. In *Satchmo: My Life in New Orleans* (1954), Armstrong reveals, "I always felt inferior to the pimps" (p. 199). Such statements document the importance of the pimps in the ghetto community, although of course they do not prove that the pimps were as much an asset to American life as creators like Armstrong. Skill in *walking that walk* (sometimes called the *Pimp Strut*) and *talking that talk* (using the slang and excelling in other typically Black aspects of verbal performance) is, by all published accounts, a requisite for a successful career in procuring.

[31] See *All-American English*, p. 163.

[32] Dalby, *op. cit.*, p. 182. Dalby cites Mandingo *jɔn*, 'a person owned by someone else'.

[33] Robert Beck ("Iceberg Slim"), *Pimp: The Story of My Life*, Holloway House, 1969. Note that Beck writes of the "master pimp who turned me out"—i.e., introduced him to the practices necessary for successful pimping. Beck and other writers on pimping use a lot of slang phrases *(pull my coat to* 'inform me of') that seem peripheral to a treatment like this because they are not a part of general Black ethnic slang.

[34] Johnson, *op. cit.*, p. 309.

[35] J. F. D. Smyth, *A Tour of the United States of America*, 1784, p. 121.

[36] William Labov, Paul Cohen, Clarence Robins, and John Lewis, *A Study of the English of Blacks and Puerto Ricans in New York City*, U.S. Office of Education Cooperative Research Project No. 3288, final report, 1968.

[37] *Ibid.*, II:164–166.

[38] Quoted in Frederic Ramsey, *Been Here and Gone*, p. 129.

[39] Marshall Stearns and Jean Stearns, *Jazz Dance,* Macmillan, 1968, pp. 24–30.

[40] *Op. cit.,* II:146.

[41] P. 285.

[42] William Smith, *A New Voyage to Guinea,* 1744, p. 53.

[43] William Labov, probably the leader of the linguists who long resisted the notion that there could be any syntactic differences between Black English and Standard English, admits this point in *Language in the Inner City,* University of Pennsylvania Press, 1972, p. 53.

[44] Probably the best-written description of this phenomenon is in Eldridge Cleaver, *Soul on Ice,* Delta, 1969.

[45] The most suggestive article on this subject is John M. Hellman's " 'I'm a Monkey,' The Influence of the Black American Blues Argot on the Rolling Stones," *Journal of American Folklore* 86 (1973):367–73. For the development of some of the onomastic suggestions of this article, see Chapter II of my *Black Names* (Mouton, forthcoming).

Chapter 8

[1] Mathew Carey, *The American Museum, or Repository,* 1787.

[2] *Monthly Magazine* XIV (Supplement 1804):626.

[3] *Works,* ed. Jared Sparks, Vol. 7:71–72.

[4] James Harvey Young, "American Medical Quackery in the Age of the Common Man," *Journal of American History* 47 (June–March 1960–61). The above material is a partial paraphrase of some of Young's materials, with certain data (especially the dates of the earliest attestations) added. Although he does not say so, Young clearly assumes that *medicine show* came into English at about the same time as the other phrases. As the discerning

reader may have perceived, one of the corollaries to the basic premise of this book is that words or expressions belonging to the same sociolinguistic domain tend to be borrowed together. This is contrary to at least two more frequently advanced theses: that "each word has its own history" and that borrowings follow settlement patterns.

⁵ Young, *passim,* documents the importance of newspaper publicity.

⁶ Katherine T. Kell, "Tobacco in Folk Cures in Western Society," *Journal of American Folklore,* Vol. 78 (April–June 1965), pp. 104–5.

⁷ Harriet van Horne, quoted in Vance Packard, *The Hidden Persuaders,* David McKay, 1957, p. 168.

⁸ Packard, *op. cit.,* p. 200. Note that, although Packard's book was originally printed in 1957, this quotation is from the 1975 version.

⁹ David Dalby, "The African Element in American English," in Thomas Kochman (ed.), *Rappin' and Stylin' Out: Communication in Urban Black America,* University of Illinois Press, 1972. Dalby cites Wolof *waw kay* or *waw ke,* Mandingo *on-ke,* Dogno *o-kay,* Djabo *o-ke,* and Western Fula *'eeyi kay,* all meaning "yes indeed." It is important that there are possible source forms in several West African languages, some of which (especially Wolof) are used as lingua francas. Borrowing from an individual language not used as a lingua franca is extremely difficult in a multilingual situation like that of American slavery. See Chapter 1 for a fuller discussion of this point concerning American Indian borrowings.

¹⁰ Hans Sperber, "Fifty-four Forty or Fight: Fact and Fictions," *American Speech* 32 (1952):5–11.

¹¹ This point, which may have a tendency to shock the reader brought up on the banalities of our school history books, emerges quite clearly from any examination of the actual records. I would recommend especially *The Life*

and Adventures of James P. Beckwourth and A. H. Favour's *Old Bill Williams, Mountain Man* (see Bibliography).

[12] B. A. Botkin, *A Treasury of American Folklore,* Crown, p. 276.

[13] This statement is based on a frequency count of such terms in the *New Yorker* for ten issues each in 1934 and 1974. The same count shows a remarkable increase in the use of compounds in clothing advertisements.

Bibliography

Abenethy, Francis Edward (ed.). *The Folklore of Texas Cultures,* Austin, Texas, The Encino Press, 1974.

Adair, James. *The History of the American Indians* (ed. Samuel Cole Williams), New York, Promontory Press, 1930.

Adams, Ramon F. *Western Words,* University of Oklahoma Press, 1961 and 1968.

———. *The Rampaging Herd: A Bibliography of the Books and Pamphlets on Men and Events in the Cattle Industry,* University of Oklahoma Press, 1959.

———. *The Cowboy Says It Salty,* University of Arizona Press, 1971.

———. *The Old-Time Cowhand,* New York, Macmillan, 1961.

——— (ed. and compiler). *The Best of the Cowboy,* University of Oklahoma Press, 1957.

Allen, Harold B., and Gary N. Underwood (eds.). *Readings in American Dialectology,* New York, Appleton-Century-Crofts, 1971.

Anderson, John Q. "The New Orleans Voodoo Ritual Dance and Its Twentieth-Century Survivals," *Southern Folklore Quarterly* XXIV (1960):135–43.

Asbury, Herbert. *The Barbary Coast: An Informal History of the San Francisco Underworld,* New York, 1933.

————. *Sucker's Progress: An Informal History of Gambling in America from the Colonies to Canfield,* 1938 (reprinted Patterson Smith, Montclair, N.J., 1966).

————. *The French Quarter: An Informal History of the New Orleans Underworld,* New York, Knopf, 1936.

Babcock, C. Merton. "The Social Significance of the Language of the American Frontier," *American Speech* XXIV (1949), 256–63.

Babington, Mina, and E. Bagby Atwood. "Lexical Usage in Southern Louisiana," *Publications of the American Dialect Society* 36 (November 1961).

Barnes, W. C. *Western Grazing Grounds and Forest Ranges,* Chicago, 1913.

Barnett, Lincoln. *The Treasury of Our Tongue,* New York, Knopf, 1964.

Barsness, Larry. *Gold Camp, Alder Gulch, and Virginia City, Montana,* New York, Hastings House, 1962.

Bartlett, John Russell. *Dictionary of Americanisms,* New York, 1877.

Beck, Robert ("Iceberg Slim"). *Pimp: The Story of My Life,* Los Angeles, Holloway House, 1969.

Boas, Franz. *Handbook of American Indian Languages,* 2 vols., Anthropological Publications, Oosterhout N.B., The Netherlands, 1969.

Botkin, B. A. *A Treasury of American Folklore,* New York, Crown, 1944.

Brown, Roger. *Words and Things: An Introduction to Language,* New York, Free Press, 1958.

Chase, John. *Frenchmen, Desire, Good Children,* New Orleans, Robert L. Crager and Co., 1949.

Chopin, Kate. *Bayou Folk,* Houghton Mifflin, 1894.

————. *A Night in Acadie,* Way and Williams, 1897.

Colcord, Joanna Carver. *Sea Language Comes Ashore,* New York, 1945.

————. *Songs of American Sailormen*, New York, 1938.

Dalby, David. "The African Element in Black American English," in Kochman (ed.), *Rappin' and Stylin' Out*, University of Illinois Press, 1972.

Dellenbaugh, Frederick S. *A Canyon Voyage*, Yale University Press, 1908.

Dick, Everett N. *Vanguards of the Frontier*, New York, 1940.

————. "The Long Drive," *Collections of the Kansas Historical Society* XVII (1926–28).

————. *The Sod-House Frontier, 1854–90*, New York, 1944.

Dickens, Charles. *American Notes*, London, 1842.

————. *Martin Chuzzlewit*, London, 1844.

Dillard, J. L. *Black English: Its History and Usage in the United States*, New York, Random House, 1972.

————. *All-American English: A History of American English*, New York, Random House, 1975.

Dodge, Lieutenant Colonel Richard Irving. *The Black Hills*, New York, James Miller, 1876.

Dollard, John. *Class and Caste in a Southern Town*, New Haven, 1937.

Dorson, Richard M. *America in Legend: Folklore from the Colonial Period to the Present*, New York, Pantheon, 1973.

Dundes, Alan (ed.). *Mother Wit from the Laughing Barrel*, Englewood Cliffs, N.J., Prentice-Hall, 1972.

Earle, Alice Morse. *Customs and Fashions in Old New England*, Williamstown, Mass. 1969.

————. *Stage-Coach and Tavern Days*, New York, Macmillan, 1900.

Evans, Oliver. "Melting Pot in the Bayous," *American Heritage*, December 1963.

Everand, Wayne M. "Bourbon City, New Orleans 1874–1900," *Louisiana Studies* XI (Fall, 1972):240–51.

Farmer, John Stephen, and W. E. Henley. *Slang and Its Analogues,* New York, 1965.

Favour, A. H. *Old Bill Williams, Mountain Man,* University of North Carolina Press, 1935.

Fisher, Miles Mark. *Negro Slave Songs in the United States,* New York, The Citadel Press, 1953.

Forbes, Jack D. *The Indian in America's Past,* Englewood Cliffs, N.J., Prentice-Hall, 1962.

Foster, Brian. *The Changing English Language,* New York, 1968.

Freeman, Edward A. *Some Impressions of the United States,* 1883. .

Gayarré, Charles. "The New Orleans Bench and Bar in 1823," *Harper's Magazine,* Vol. 77 (1881).

Goedel, Gustav. *Der Deutschen Seemannssprache,* Kiel, 1902.

Gonzales, Ambrose. *The Black Border: Gullah Stories of the Carolina Coast,* Columbia, S.C., 1922.

Guthrie, Alfred Bertram. *The Big Sky,* Houghton-Mifflin, 1947.

——. *The Way West,* Sloane, 1949.

Hancock, Ian F. "Lexical Expansion Outside a Closed System," *Journal of African Languages* XII (1973).

Holt, Alfred H. *Phrase Origins,* New York, 1936.

Hotten, J. C. *The Slang Dictionary,* London, 1887.

Hubbard, Claude. "Language of Ruxton's Mountain Men," *American Speech,* October, 1968: 216–221.

Hymes, Dell (ed.). *Pidginization and Creolization of Languages,* Cambridge University Press, 1971.

Indian Talk: Hand Signals of the American Indian. Healdsburg, California, Naturegraph Publishers, 1970.

Jones, Richard Foster. *The Triumph of the English Language,* Stanford University Press, 1953.

Kahane, Henry, Renee Kahane, and Andreas Tietze. *The*

Lingua Franca in the Levant: Turkish Nautical Terms of Italian and Greek Origin, Urbana, University of Illinois Press, 1958.

Kane, Harnett. *The Bayous of Louisiana,* New York, William Morrow, 1943.

————. *Deep Delta Country,* New York, Duell, Sloan, and Pearce, 1944.

————. *Natchez on the Mississippi,* New York, William Morrow, 1947.

————. *Queen New Orleans: City by the River,* New York, 1949.

Katzenbach, Edward L., Jr. "Poker, Pawns, and Politics," in Neil Postman, Charles Weingartner, and Terence P. Moran (eds.), *Language in America,* New York, Pegasus, 1969.

Kell, Katherine T. "Folk Names for Tobacco," *Journal of American Folklore* 79 (1966):590–99.

Keyes, Francis Parkinson. *Dinner at Antoine's,* New York, 1948.

Kime, Wayne R. "Washington Irving and Frontier Speech," *American Speech,* February 1967, 5–19.

Kochman, Thomas (ed.). *Rappin' and Stylin' Out: Communication in Urban Black America,* University of Illinois Press, 1972.

Krapp, George Philip. *The English Language in America,* New York, 1925.

Labov, William, Clarence Robins, Paul Cohen, and John Lewis. *A Study of the Non-Standard English of Negro and Puerto Rican Speakers in New York City,* Columbia University, mimeographed, 1968.

Life and Adventures of James P. Beckwourth, Mountaineer, Scout Pioneer, and Chief of the Crow Nation of Indians. New York, Harper and Row, 1856.

Leech, Geoffrey N. *English in Advertising,* London, Longmans, 1966.

Marckwardt, Albert. *American English,* New York, 1958.

Marryat, Captain Frederick. *Diary in America* (ed. Jules Zanger), Indiana University Press, 1960.

Martineau, Harriet. *Retrospect of Western Travel,* London, Saunders and Ottley, 1838.

Mathews, Mitford M. *American Words,* The World Publishing Co., Cleveland, 1959.

————. *Beginnings of American English,* University of Chicago Press, 1931.

Matsell, George W. *Vocabularium, or the Rogue's Lexicon,* New York, 1859.

Mencken, Henry Louis. *The American Language,* New York, 1919. Second Edition, 1921. Third Edition, 1923. Fourth Edition, 1936. Supplement One, 1945. Supplement Two, 1948.

Morgan, Murray. *Skid Road: An Informal Portrait of Seattle,* New York, Viking, 1960.

Nathan, Hans. *Dan Emmett and the Rise of Early Negro Minstrelsy,* University of Oklahoma Press, 1964.

Needler, Geoffrey D. "Linguistic Evidence from Alexander Hamilton's *Itinerarium,*" *American Speech* October 1967.

Newman, Edwin. *Strictly Speaking: Will America Be the Death of English?* Indianapolis, Bobbs-Merrill Co., 1974.

O'Brien, Esse F. *The First Bulldogger,* San Antonio, Texas, The Naylor Company, 1961.

Ogg, Frederic Austin. *The Opening of the Mississippi: A Struggle for Supremacy in the American Interior,* New York, Macmillan, 1904.

Oliver, Paul. *Blues Fell This Morning,* London, Hertford and Harlow, 1960.

Orth, Samuel P. *Our Forefathers: A Chronicle of Americans in the Making,* New Haven, 1920.

Osgood, Cornelius. *Linguistic Structures of Native America,* New York, 1946.

Packard, Vance. *The Hidden Persuaders,* New York, David McKay, 1957.

Parkman, Francis. *The Oregon Trail, Sketches of Prairie and Rocky Mountain Life,* Boston, Little, Brown and Company, 1872.

Partridge, Eric, and John W. Clark. *British and American English Since 1900,* London, 1951.

Porter, Kenneth Wiggins. *The Negro on the American Frontier,* New York, Arno Press, 1971.

Power, Tyrone, Esq. *Impressions of America During the Years 1833, 1834, and 1835,* London, 1836.

Prince, J. Dyneley. "An Ancient New Jersey Indian Jargon," *American Anthropologist* 14:508.

———. "Jersey Dutch," *Dialect Notes,* 1910.

Pringle, Henry Fowles. *Theodore Roosevelt,* Harcourt, 1931.

Ramsey, Carolyn. *Cajuns on the Bayou,* New York, 1957.

Ramsey, Frederic, Jr. *Been Here and Gone,* New Brunswick, N.J., Rutgers University Press, 1960.

Richardson, Albert D. *Beyond the Mississippi: From the Great River to the Great Ocean, Life and Adventure in the Prairies, Mountains, and Pacific Coast,* Hartford, 1867.

Read, William A. *Louisiana French,* Louisiana State University Press, 1963.

Reisman, Karl. "Cultural and Linguistic Ambiguity in a West Indian Village," in Norman E. Whitten and John Szwed (eds.), *Afro-American Anthropology: Contemporary Perspectives,* New York, Free Press, 1970.

Rollins, Philip Ashton. *The Cowboy: An Unconventional History of Civilization on the Old-Time Cattle Range,* New York, Charles Scribner's Sons, 1936.

Rusling, James F. *Across America; or, the Great West,* New York, 1875.

Ruxton, George Frederick. *Life in the Far West,* 1848.

Safire, William. *New Language of Politics: An Anecdotal Dictionary of Catchwords, Slogans, and Political Usage,* New York, Random House, 1968.

Saxon, Lyle. *Fabulous New Orleans,* Robert Craft and Co., 1928.

————. *Old Louisiana,* New Orleans, Robert Craft and Co., 1929.

———— and Robert Tallant. *Gumbo Ya-Ya,* Louisiana Writers' Project, 1945.

Schur, Norman W. *British Self-Taught, with Comments in American,* New York, Macmillan, 1973.

Searight, Sarah. *New Orleans,* New York, Stein and Day, 1973.

Skinner, Constance L. *Adventurers of Oregon: A Chronicle of the Fur Trade,* Yale University Press, 1920.

Smith, Logan Pearsall. *Words and Idioms: Studies in the English Language,* Boston, Houghton Mifflin Co., 1925.

Smith, Page. *John Adams,* Garden City, N.Y., Doubleday, 1924.

Sonneck, O. G. T. *Report on the Star-Spangled Banner, Hail Columbia, America, and Yankee Doodle,* Washington, D.C., 1909.

Stewart, William A. "On the Use of Negro Dialect in the Teaching of Reading," in Joan Baratz and Roger Shuy (eds.), *Teaching Black Children to Read,* Washington, D.C., 1969.

Trennet, John. *The Poor Planters Physician,* Williamsburg, Virginia, 1734.

Trelease, Allen W. *Indian Affairs in Colonial New York,* Cornell University Press, 1960.

Trittschuh, Travis. "Words and Phrases in American Politics: 'Boom'," *American Speech* 31 (1956):172–79.

Trollope, Mrs. Frances. *Domestic Manners of the Americans* (ed. Donald Smalley), New York, Vintage Books, 1949.

Van Loon, L. G. *Crumbs from an Old Dutch Closet,* The Hague, 1938.

Vogel, Virgil J. *American Indian Medicine,* Norman, Oklahoma, 1970.

Ward, Christopher. *The War of the Revolution,* New York, Macmillan, 1952.

Warburton, Austen D. *Indian Lore of the North California Coast,* Santa Clara, California, Pacific Pueblo Press, 1966.

Whitman, Walt. "Slang in America," *The North American Review,* Vol. 141 (1885).

Winslow, Ola Elizabeth. *John Eliot, Apostle to the Indians,* Boston, 1968.

Wise, Claude M. "Specimen of Louisiana French-English; or Cajun Dialect in Phonetic Transcription," *American Speech* 8 (1933):63–64.

———. "Louisiana Speech Under Many Flags," *Southern Speech Journal* 4 (1939):8–13.

Wister, Fanny Kemble (ed.). *Owen Wister Out West,* The University of Chicago Press, 1958.

Wolfram, Walter. "The Relationship of White Southern Speech to Vernacular Black English," *Language* 50 (1974): 498–527.

Wood, Gordon R. *Vocabulary Change: A Study of Variation in Regional Words in Eight of the Southern States,* Southern Illinois University Press, Carbondale and Edwardsville, 1971.

Young, James Harvey. "American Medical Quackery in the Age of the Common Man," *Journal of American History* 47 (1960–61).

Index

About the Author

J. L. DILLARD is a linguistics teacher, researcher, and writer who has taught in many universities in the United States and abroad, including Universidad Central in Ecuador, Université Officielle de Bujumbura in Burundi, Ferkauf Graduate School of Yeshiva University in New York City, and the University of Puerto Rico. He now teaches at Northwestern State University in Natchitoches, Louisiana.

AMERICAN TALK

Jargon, teachers of English composition keep telling us, is something to be avoided. Yet, as J. L. Dillard cheerfully demonstrates in this book, it is jargon, more than anything else, that makes American English different from British, and American jargon has a rich and varied history.

In keeping with the traditions of our country, American jargon comes from our multilingual background, our vices—smoking, drinking, gambling—and our occupations, from fur-trapping to politics.

American Indians gave us—in addition to *powwow, mugwump* and *bury the hatchet—here's how, big mouth* and *fireworks.* From the influential early Dutch settlers we got, along with many other words, *dollar, cookie, dope* (in the sense of *dope peddler* or *dope sheet*) and *boom.* Out of the pidgin English that developed from the efforts of Dutch, English, French and Indians to converse together came, among numerous familiar phrases, *no go.* Poker, that most American of all games, provided *just for openers, pass the buck, call the turn, break even, four-flusher* and *deal,* as both a noun and a verb. American drinking habits produced not only *cocktail* and *cob-*